Guidestones
Great Langdale Ax

Ancient ways to stone axe working sites

in the

English Lake District

Gabriel M Blamires

First published in the United Kingdom in 2005 by:
Gabriel M Blamires, 114 Greenacres, Wetheral, Carlisle, Cumbria, England.

email:
gabrielblamires@tinywold.co.uk

British Library Cataloguing in Publication Data

A catalogue record for this book is available from the British Library.

ISBN 0-9550270-0-4

Photographs: Gabriel Blamires

The maps on pages 18, 37, 38, 56, 74, 90, and 106 are based on reproductions of the 1920 Ordnance Survey 6 inches to 1 mile map for Westmorland, Sheet XXV NE. The map on page 120 is based on a reproduction of the 1947 Ordnance Survey 1 inch to the mile map, No 82 (Keswick).

Printed and bound in the United Kingdom by Colophon Press Printers Ltd, Carlisle

Cover Photo: Pike o' Stickle, with the The Pike o' Stickle pentagon (stone number 4.5 in the text) in the foreground

CONTENTS

List of Maps

Tables

Acknowledgements

It is a pleasure to take this opportunity to record thanks to a number of people who have helped towards the production of this book. Thanks are especially due:

- to James Quartermaine, Project Manager, Oxford Archaeology North, for his much valued critical appraisal of the book at draft stage;

- to Philip Holdsworth, former Cumbria County Archaeologist; Bette Hopkins, formerly Cumbria County Council Sites and Monuments Records Officer; and the staff of Carlisle Library for responding so willingly to my enquiries;

- to Richard Hall, former Hon. Sec. of the Cumberland and Westmorland Antiquarian and Archaeological Society; and Tom Clare, for feedback on an early draft;

- to Professors Barry Cunliffe and Richard Bradley for their feedback on an early draft text;

- to Steve Parkhouse for his advice on design and presentation at an early stage;

- to my father for his advice in knocking successive drafts into some sort of intelligible shape;

- and to my wife Magna, who has tolerated so patiently my persistent preoccupation with old stones dotted about the Cumbrian landscape.

In expressing these grateful thanks, I need to make it clear that those who have given such valuable support do not necessarily share my views on the particular interpretation of the megaliths set out in these pages – for these I alone am responsible.

Gabriel Blamires

Preface

These days we are all accustomed to see sign 'posts' to point us on our way, as we travel about the countryside. In many parts of the English Lake District landscape, certain large stones – 'megaliths' – occur, with a distinctive characteristic: they are shaped so as to point in significant directions. In this book it is suggested that these megaliths performed a function similar to modern signposts – as signs in stone, to point the way in ancient times.

Such stones, which appear to be unworked apart from their distinct points, are often spaced out in succession over considerable distances. In general, they appear up to now to have remained unnoticed. This book presents the first published account of a sample of such megaliths in Great Langdale. They apparently mark prehistoric ways along the valley, and up to Neolithic axe making sites in the Langdale Pikes (the so-called Great Langdale axe factories).

The use of standing stones and other stones to mark prehistoric paths is not unknown. This book breaks new ground, however, in demonstrating the use of stones with certain shapes in profile, or on their upper surfaces, which were apparently intended to act as pointers or guidestones indicating a direction. A number of such likely guidestones are identified for the first time, together with the probable course of the path followed by the Neolithic stone axe makers up Great Langdale; and some ways to the axe making sites, as revealed by such stones.

Some readers may plan to explore in the field the routes to the stone axe 'factories' described in this book. The actual stone axe working sites lie on land high up in the Pikes, owned by the National Trust. They constitute a precious and fragile part of our archaeological heritage and should not of course be disturbed in any way without permission from the Trust.

This book provides an important new perspective on Lake District routes in prehistoric times; and on prehistoric lines of communication in general. It will be of interest to archaeologists, antiquarians, and all those who are curious about ancient megaliths, ancient trackways and the Great Langdale stone axe factories; and also to visitors and ramblers keen to explore ancient ways and antiquities in the beautiful Langdales.

PART 1
THE GREAT LANGDALE WAY

1 INTRODUCTION

Long ago – perhaps 4,500 years ago or more – the Neolithic people seem to have made use of large stones (megaliths) as guidestones, to point their way through the Lake District. They chose megaliths which displayed shapes similar to those which appear in many of the individual stones in the surviving stone circles of Cumbria. However, unlike the stones in those circles, such megalithic guidestone features have, until now, rested silent and unrecognized in the Lakeland landscape.

This new thesis is illustrated in the following pages by reference to a known Neolithic communication link: a route along the Great Langdale valley and up to the extensive Neolithic stone axe workings high in the Pikes (the so-called Great Langdale axe factories). The authorities agree in the main that such a route in this general direction must have existed; although the exact line or elevation of the path has not up to now been identified [1].

In the present chapter, some brief background details on Great Langdale Neolithic stone axe production and distribution are sketched in; together with outline evidence on Neolithic pathways in general, and the Neolithic use of megaliths as waymarks. In chapters 2 to 4, megaliths apparently pointing the way at intervals along the Great Langdale valley are described. In chapters 5 to 7, further megaliths which appear to point ways up from the valley to the axe working sites, are explored.

Chapter 8 draws together some conclusions. Two significant results emerge. Firstly, the material provides a demonstration, in this sample area, of the likely use of megalithic waymarks by the Neolithic people to point their routes; the types of stone they used, and the preferred locations, are described. Secondly, routes apparently followed by the Neolithic people from the SE along Great Langdale, and up to the axe working sites, are for the first time identified in some detail.

The making of Neolithic stone axes in Cumbria

The making and distribution of Great Langdale stone axes provides the context for this exploration. The coast of Cumbria – the west and south west coastal lowlands in particular – bear witness to the presence of people there from Mesolithic times. It is possible that the people from the coastal areas who followed a Mesolithic way of life may have been the first to fashion stone axes from the Borrowdale tuff of Scafell Pike and the Langdale Pikes [2].

From about 3800 BC pollen analysis has shown an elm decline in the coastal lowlands, suggesting that clearances for farming (assuming that no pest like the Dutch elm disease of

Pike o' Stickle

Extensive stone axe working sites have been found on the buttresses of Pike o' Stickle, on the screes below and on the neighbouring crags.

modern times was responsible for this decline) [3]. Pollen analysis also shows episodic woodland clearance in the Langdale Combe and Blea Tarn areas from about 3800 BC [4]. This suggests penetration into the Langdales by Neolithic immigrant farmers, for summer seasonal grazing of animal herds. From about the same time, people probably from the coastal lowlands, began to exploit the sources of Borrowdale volcanic tuff on Scafell Pike, Glaramara, and especially the Langdale Pikes, for the making of stone axes. *Bradley's* excavations at axe working sites give dates of around 3650 BC for activity at a site on the Harrison path; 3570 BC for a site on Stake Beck; and 3530 BC and 3330 BC for working sites on the Pike o' Stickle top buttress [5]. *Clough's* excavations at Thunacar Knott produced a date of about 2524 BC [6]. For a span of many centuries – up to one thousand five hundred years - axes continued to be made in stone originating from the vicinity of the Pikes [7].

For the first four hundred years or so, the finished products appear to have been made to satisfy the needs of the people within the local region in the lowland periphery of the Lake District. Three hundred years later than on the coast - from about 3500 BC - woodland clearance began in the Eden Valley, indicating Neolithic settlement in the area; and it is possible that the Eden Valley settlers came from Yorkshire, where there was a big Neolithic population and power base [8].

After this Neolithic settlement of the Eden valley, the Langdale Pikes rose to importance as the premier source of stone for polished stone axes, which were distributed through much of Britain. The axes from this source (Group VI) began to be taken to more distant parts from about 3400 BC, and this trend increased to a peak around 3000 BC [9]. At the Great Langdale sites, the making of stone axes for transmission to distant parts, appears to have continued to flourish until about 2500 BC [10]. After this, with the introduction of bronze axes into Britain, the activity at the Great Langdale axe making sites seems to have declined sharply; ceasing altogether by about 2300 BC, and possibly earlier [11].

The painstaking and detailed survey by *Claris and Quartermaine* revealed numerous distinct chipping sites, particularly in the Langdale Pikes, where the stone was chipped into roughout axes [12].

Long distance axe trading, giving, or exchange

When first discovered, the Pike o' Stickle axe working site was dubbed a 'factory', and this label has stuck. The language of modern economics has been further applied by some commentators, to suggest a 'trade' undertaken by 'middle men' to communities far off; with 'bulk transport' and a 'redistribution centre' on Humberside [13].

The comparative knowledge that we have of more recent primitive societies suggests that it may be inappropriate to apply the language and concepts of modern industrial production and commerce to Neolithic communities. The actual processes by which axes were traded, exchanged or gifted to people in distant parts are not known. It seems likely that exchange of stone axes formed part of wider social and ceremonial interrelationships and activities – not merely economic ones – including relationships between one Regional

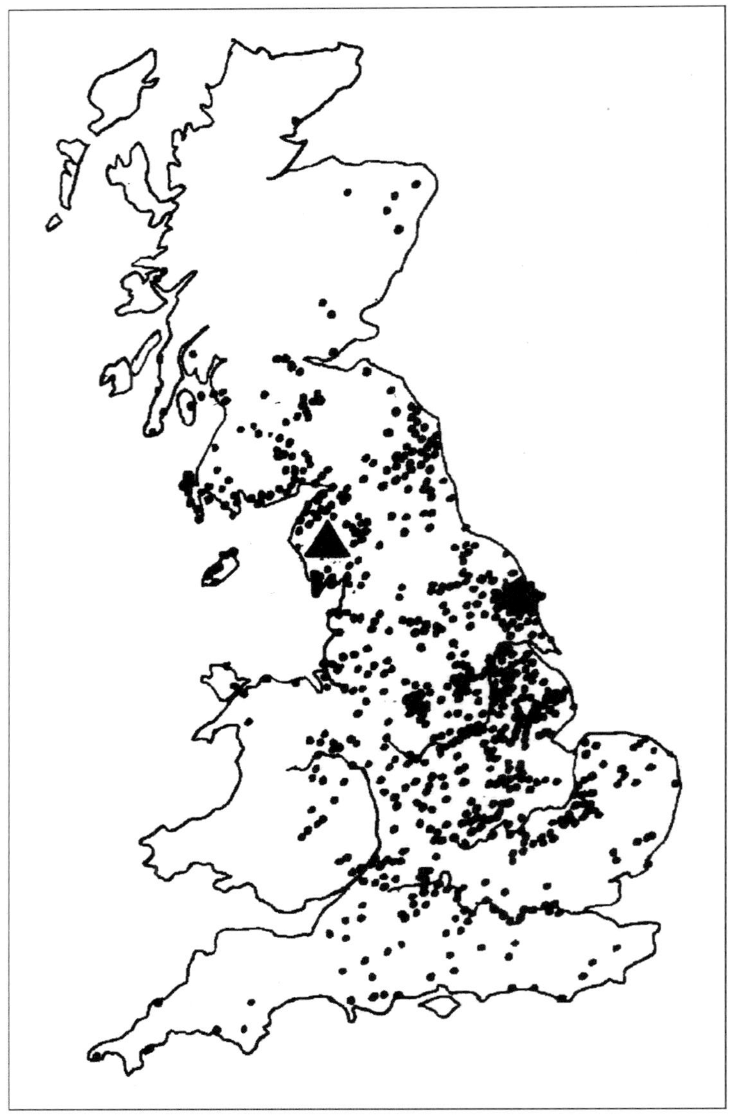

Map indicating the variations in density of distribution of finds of Great Langdale stone axes in mainland Britain. The Great Langdale axe making site is marked with a black triangle.
(After Clough and Cummins, 1988)

community and another; and that axes reached East Yorkshire, the Midlands and further south by successive interactions of this kind [14].

More stone axes have been identified as deriving from the Great Langdale source, than from any other stone axe source in Britain. The axes recovered are numbered in thousands. They have turned up in a wide distribution over much of Britain. Whilst the axes have been found in moderate numbers around the lowland periphery of the Lake District, occurrences locally within the fells of the Lake District are sparse. To the north, axes have been discovered in significant numbers in SW Scotland and Northumberland. To the south, the finds extend along the Lancashire coast and up the River Ribble. To the west, Cumbrian axes have been picked up in the Isle of Man, and a few reached Ireland.

The strongest concentrations of finds of Group VI axes are to be found, however, at substantial distances away SE in Yorkshire. The heaviest concentrations of all occur in the Bridlington and Flamborough Head areas of East Yorkshire (although finds have been sparse in the intervening Pennines); and substantial numbers of discoveries continue south of the Humber in areas bordering the River Trent – the Lincolnshire Wolds and Nottinghamshire, extending into the Peak District. Further finds are concentrated in the areas bordering the Rivers Welland, Nene and Ouse draining into the Wash; and the Thames and Severn [15].

Evidence of communication routes

Well defined routes would have been established, by which axes were conveyed from the axe stone sources, perhaps from one community to another, to the eventual destination areas. Where did these routes lie? Evidence in the form of known trackways is conspicuous by its absence. Curiously, in spite of centuries of long distance transmission of Langdale axes to other parts of the country, little trace of the actual pathways which were followed from the axe stone sources has up to now been identified. In the following pages new evidence is presented to suggest the beginnings of a route from a SE direction to the stone axe working sites in Great Langdale.

A few outline features of Neolithic ways in general may be identified. There was no need for a paved or cobbled surface - the Neolithic people had no wheeled transport; nor did they ride horses. It is thought that in some places the routes of this period consisted of broad bands of parallel paths, rather than one single well defined track [16]. In others it seems likely that no definite 'path' or 'track' may have existed at all – there would have simply been an undefined 'way' as often existed in Medieval times. It may be safer to envisage Neolithic 'ways' having these characteristics, rather than to presuppose that there would always have been a single worn down path or track.

The association of the wider distribution of Cumbrian stone axes with navigable rivers such as the Ribble, Humber, Trent and Thames is very marked [17]. For the most part the fast flowing, rock strewn rivers of Cumbria do not lend themselves to navigation; but this need not have prevented the Neolithic people from sticking to their habit of following the river valleys, on foot rather than by boat. Once the lakes and the sea coasts were reached,

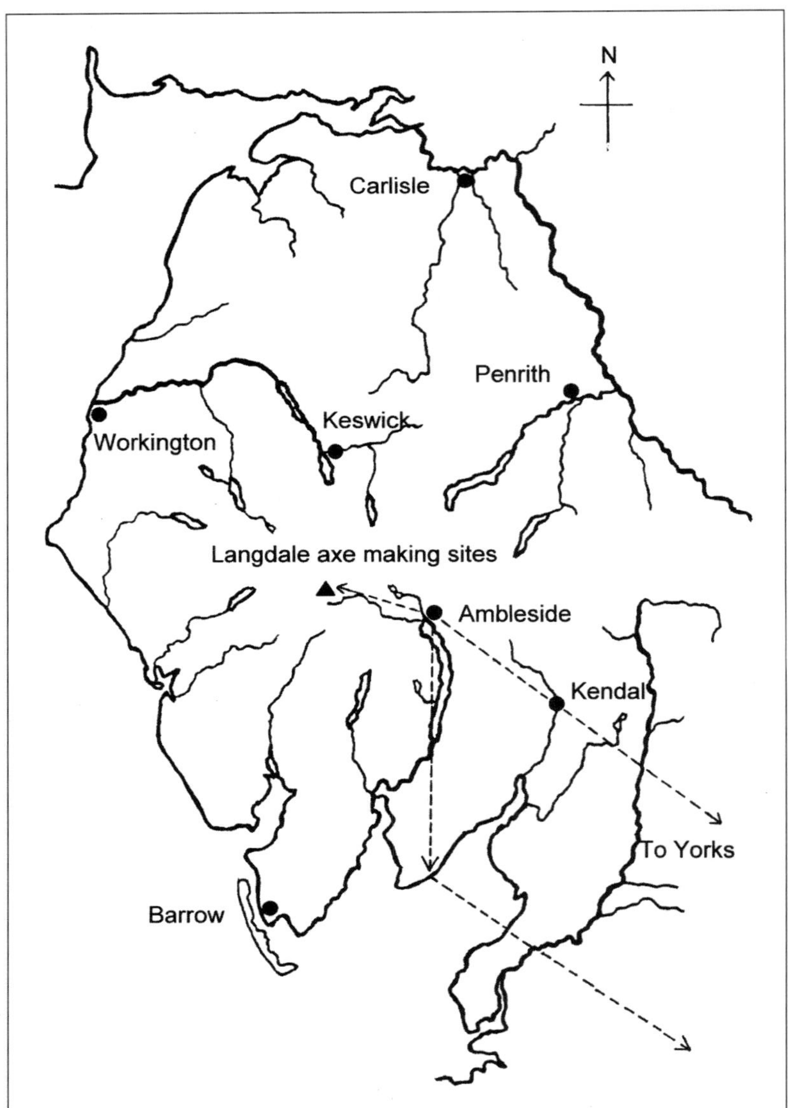

Map of Cumbria showing two possible routes which have been suggested for the transmission of stone axes from Great Langdale to East Yorkshire

it is likely that the axes were taken by boat on their onward journeys up and down the west coasts of Britain. It is thought that the people of those times took to the sea in boats made of skin stretched over simple frames, like Irish curraghs. Dugouts may also have been used in calmer inland waters [18].

There must have been a much travelled route, or routes, linking communities in East Yorkshire with those nearer the Lakeland axe working sites. Roughouts of the axe heads were made at the axe stone sources, and then these roughouts were taken down to lowland sites for grinding and polishing into the finished products. Although no actual grinding and polishing sites have yet been identified in the Yorkshire direction, finds of stray roughouts provide evidence as to where Neolithic travellers from the axe stone sources passed by.

Several roughout discoveries support the hypothesis of a SE route or routes (among others) away from the axe making sites. In Great Langdale itself, beyond the axe working sites, the butt-end of a Neolithic chisel was found at Robin Gill [19]. Outside the mouth of the valley, a large roughout axe was discovered at Loughrigg Tarn, and another at High Close, just above the tarn [20]. Further SE, roughout finds occur at Troutbeck; at Underscar towards Kendal; and on the Lancashire side of Morecambe Bay [21]. Whilst they occur only rarely still further afield, such rare examples include, significantly, three finds in Yorkshire at Skipton, Keighley and Malton [22].

Stone circles may also offer clues as to Neolithic communications routes. *Aubrey Burl* noted that the early Cumbrian henges and stone circles were situated along the stone axe trade routes [23]. There was a circle at Hirdwood, near the head of the Troutbeck valley (which runs NNE from the east side of Lake Windermere), giving access to High Street and Kirkstone Pass. It could be significant that a Cumbrian roughout axe was found in the vicinity [24]. Further SE, to the NE of Kirkby Lonsdale, an impressive embanked stone circle lies at Casterton [25]. The dimensions and stylistic characteristics of these two stone circles did not lead Burl to classify them amongst the early stone circles. However, the roughout find is suggestive of an early date for Hirdwood. No direct dating evidence has been found for the Casterton circle, and an early date for this one is also possible.

Whilst travel by ridgeways appears to have been favoured in the Bronze Age, some known precedents suggest that the Neolithic people before them seem to have preferred to travel along the sides of valleys or escarpments, rather than on the ridge tops. One illustration of this is the Icknield Way, which passes along the north side of the Chilterns [26]; and the Pilgrims' Way, lying along the south side of the North Downs, is another [27]. Such pathways have been deduced to have existed in Neolithic times from the extensive Neolithic sites and finds along their routes.

More clues to the beginnings of the pathways followed by the axe makers are to be found near the main axe stone sources in the Pikes. In the vicinity of the main working sites, but detached a little way from them along paths through the fells still used today, outlying small working sites suggest the initial directions of arterial routes. *Claris and*

Quartermaine identified some such working sites (type D) – typically shallow deposits of debitage detached from the primary stone sources. Although relatively minor in terms of production volume, they tend to be situated along ways giving natural access to the main working sites. They could indicate the beginnings of the routes by which the roughouts were taken from the production areas [28]. In the south eastern direction (with which we are concerned in these pages), some such sites lay down the Thorn Crag path down to Mark Gate; and along the Harrison path leading down towards Pike Howe. In considering the issue as to whether a high route or low route was taken along the valleys, it is significant that these working sites lie on paths which lead down towards the valley floor, and not to the ridges beside the valley.

Such small outlying sites were also found in the vicinity of Stickle Tarn. This suggests that the Neolithic axe stone workers may have taken advantage of the more gently sloping and slightly sheltered ground around Stickle Tarn to set up temporary camps and working sites [29].

The East Yorkshire route

Over the years since the Great Langdale axe 'factories' were discovered in the late 1940s, several commentators have put forward hypotheses as to the routes by which the axes from this source were distributed.

The natural geography of the Lake District would have strongly influenced the routes to be taken to and from the axe stone sources. Commentators from Wordsworth onwards have noted the way in which valleys radiate outwards from the central Lake District fells; and these valleys are likely to have been used by the Neolithic people travelling to and from the axe stone sources. This still leaves the question as to whether high routes were taken along the ridges beside the valleys; or low routes along the valley floors or the lower sides of the valleys. In the Cumbrian context, it is worth noting that the high erratic fell tops lining the sides of Lakeland valleys present a considerably less attractive proposition for the traveller than the gentle, rolling upland ridges of southern England.

Clare Fell was one who suggested that four valleys radiating from the central Lake District could have provided natural routes by which the roughout axes might have been carried away to be finished at more permanent settlements. One of these was the Great Langdale valley, leading on via Windermere and the River Leven to South Cumbria. She remarked on the extent to which coastal trade and penetration inland by river valleys were reflected in finds of finished axes on the Lancashire side of Morecambe Bay, and from the mouth of the Ribble at Freckleton, through Preston to Pendle and Whalley way upstream [30]. She also suggested the Aire gap, or Stainmore, or the Tyne/Irthing gap as possible trans Pennine routes, but noted that there was little evidence on this point [31].

T Manby focused on the distribution of Great Langdale axes in an article of 1965 [32]. He proposed two likely long distance routes by which axes could have been traded to the Yorkshire Wolds.

One route, which he called a "Central Pennine Route", builds on the observations of Clare Fell. It lies as follows:

> Across Morecambe Bay by boat into the Wyre Estuary
> Overland across the Fylde to cross the Ribble at Preston
> Along the south side of Ribblesdale to the south side of the Aire Gap; **or** across the high pass between Colne and Keighley
> East along Rombald's Way to the Leeds area
> NE on to Tadcaster; then along the crest of the Escrick Moraine (a natural causeway across the marshy and forested Vale of York) to the Yorkshire Wolds.

Another likely route Manby labelled the "Craven Route", as follows:

> From lower Lonsdale and the limestone of the Craven Fault eastward
> Across the Ribble above Settle
> Across the Wharfe near Grassington
> Via Hebden and Heathfield Moors and Nidderdale
> Over Dallowgill Moor to the Ure east of Ripon
> Across the Swale near Topcliffe to the western end of the Howarden Hills
> Across the north crest of these to the Yorkshire Wolds.

W.A. Cummins envisaged a route similar to Manby's Craven route, which lay overland WNW from the source of the Aire in Yorkshire to Great Langdale: "The route to the axe factories was most probably up the River Aire to its source, over into Ribblesdale, and then by way of Settle, Ingleton, Kirkby Lonsdale, Kendal and Ambleside into Great Langdale" [33]. The natural geography certainly favours this direct route, much of which is followed today by the A 65 trunk road. However the evidence of grinding floors, settlements, henges, and early stone circles, which might indicate staging posts, is lacking.

Several different long distance routes for the transmission of Great Langdale stone axes to East Yorkshire have thus been suggested over the years. A discussion of the pros and cons of the different long distant routes which have been suggested, lies outside the scope of this book. What matters in the present context, is that the hypothesized routes share an *important common feature*: the identification of the initial section of the route as lying from the Pikes down Great Langdale to the head of Windermere. This still leaves a question as to whether the axes were carried by a high route along the ridges on the north side of the valley to Loughrigg, (the low fell at the head of Windermere); or along the valley at a lower level. There is not much doubt, however, that the people of Neolithic times used a route at some level along Great Langdale.

The use of megaliths as waymarks

To the areas of evidence so far described as to the pathways followed to and from the stone axe working sites, this study adds one further source of empirical evidence – the evidence of megaliths which present the appearance of waymarks.

A slanting *triangular* stone, close by a *pentagonal* one on its side, on the trackway past Graig Llwyd

Two stones of modest height, which have been identified as standing stones, and which show *triangular* pointed tops, on the trackway past Moel Goedog

The people of the Neolithic age specialised in the exploitation of stone - not only for the making of stone axes and other tools, but also on a much grander scale in the manipulation and erection of huge stones to create megalithic monuments. It appears that the particular stones erected in the great stone circles of Cumbria may have had other significance. In the following pages observation data is provided to show that they also appear to have used such large stones to mark their communication routes. A major way up Great Langdale to the axe working sites, together with junction routes, seems to be indicated by a series of megalithic stone waymarks.

Precedents exist elsewhere for the use of standing stones as route markers. For example, the celebrated avenues winding away from Avebury stone circle in Wiltshire were lined by great standing stones – some of which still stand today. In Cumbria, a similar avenue was once associated with stone circles at the village of Shap – although only a handful of megaliths now remain to tell the tale.

However, many of the stones identified in the following pages could not be described as 'standing' stones. For this too, there are precedents. The remains of avenues of stones at the Lacra stone circles, north of Millom contain stones that are not standing. The stones that mark an avenue sweeping up to the Kirk at Kirby Moor are not standing stones - indeed, they hardly protrude above the surface of the moorland turf.

A number of examples are also known of single lines of stones stretching over considerable distances, rather than double rows in the form of avenues. *Michael W. Taylor* noted several such alignments in an early contribution to the Transactions of the Cumberland and Westmorland Antiquarian and Archaeological Society. One example was an alignment from Newton Reigny, near Penrith, in a SW direction by Mossthorn with its long cairns, over Pallett Hill to Newbiggin.

He also recorded a local tradition that a single row of stones extended all the way from Shap (from the end of the stone circle and avenue complex which once stood there), to Moordivock above Ullswater - an area where Early Bronze Age stone circles, cairn circles and cairns are found - a distance of over five miles [34].

In Wales, tall standing stones have often been identified as route markers [35]. However, examples also occur in Wales of the use of more modest stones to mark ancient ways. In the same period that stone axes were being produced from Great Langdale, another important axe stone source was being exploited at Graig Llwyd in North Wales. A Late Neolithic/Early Bronze Age trackway, indicated by a series of stone waymarks, has long been recognized here, taking an east west route up the ridge behind the axe chipping site and past a substantial stone circle – the Druids' Circle – and several ring cairns [36]. Besides occasional standing stones marking the trackways in this area, a line of more modest stones can also be picked out in places on the way up from the west.

Another surviving example in North Wales, near Harlech, is relevant. From Llanfair, south of Harlech, on the west coast, a minor road runs NNE uphill past two Bronze Age ring cairns and a small iron age fort at Moel Goedog and on to Eisingrug. Running NNE, first along the line of the road, then along the track through the cairn circles and past the fort, archaeologists have identified an ancient way from two tall standing stones along the road to the SSW, and five further stones spaced out along from the junction of the track NNE past the fort [37].

Whilst the first standing stone is 1.7m high, and the second one over 2m high, the remaining five stones identified are of more modest size. The lowest is only 0.7m high. Two at least could be more appropriately described as sitting blocks rather than standing stones. These both have diamond shaped upper surfaces pointing in the same direction WNW to the coast above Harlech.

The significant points from these Welsh examples are, firstly, that stones other than tall standing pillars or slabs appear along the way. In general, only tall standing stones have in the past been identified by archaeologists as possible route markers. If other shapes and sizes of stones were used by the people of the Late Neolithic/Early Bronze Age to mark ways in Wales, there seems no obvious reason why the same practice should not have been adopted by their counterparts in the fells of the Lake District. Secondly, two blocks have been mentioned above which repeat a similar shape in their upper surface: the shape of a diamond. The diamond shape is a feature of prehistoric art that is displayed, for example, in the famous Neolithic tomb at New Grange in Ireland. It occurs as one of the characteristic shapes of Neolithic arrowheads. It is a shape that lends itself to use as a directional pointer.

The distinguishing characteristics of megalithic guidestones

The question arises, if stones other than standing stones were used to mark Late Neolithic/Early Bronze Age ways, by what characteristics may such stones be identified?

It is important to understand that the present study does *not* deal with alignments in the sense of stone 'rows', as interpreted by *Aubrey Burl*. Burl's book "From Carnac to Callanish" is concerned with ceremonial monuments, not guidestones marking Neolithic pathways. Indeed, his definition excludes megaliths of the type identified in these pages.

"A stone row is a prehistoric linear setting of regularly spaced standing stones, closely set, uninterrupted by any other structure. It may lead to a cairn or stone circle but the standing stones alone are the essential components of the row." [38]

The stones described in the present study do not fall within this definition of stone rows adopted by Burl. They are not necessarily *regularly* placed. They are not limited to *standing* stones. Often they cannot be described as *closely set.* They are not associated with *cairns or stone circles*. We are not dealing with stones that are necessarily closely aligned in a straight line, one with another.

No less than four stones with *triangular* profiles stand out prominently in this view of Castlerigg stone circle.

A recumbent *lozenge* shaped stone at Swinside stone circle.

This standing stone at Swinside displays a *pentagon* shaped top.

Clues may be found closer to home in the early stone circles of Cumbria, rather than in stone rows further afield. They appear to have been built over a similar period to that during which the Great Langdale axe production flourished, although some stone circles may post date the period of stone axe production. Aubrey Burl's book "The Stone Circles of the British Isles" is helpful here in distinguishing the characteristics of early and late stone circles. The large number of stones, large diameters and open centres of three of Cumbria's finest stone circles are thought to indicate that they belong to the early phase of stone circle construction – contemporaneous with the major period of stone axe production. These circles are Long Meg and her Daughters, at Little Salkeld in the Eden Valley; Castlerigg, near Keswick; and Sunkenkirk, at Swinside, north of Millom [39].

These circles, like many others in Britain, have been subject to intense examination of various kinds over the last two centuries. For example, their exact shapes, the heights of the stones, their elevations, and solar, lunar and astronomical alignments have all been studied; and searches have been undertaken for such features as underground water courses, and even magnetic currents. What has not figured prominently in the published literature, is a classification of the shapes of the stones used, and their types - what might be called a morphology of the stones. A detailed analysis would provide enough material for a book in itself. In the present context, some elementary points may be noted. When the shapes of the individual stones in these Cumbrian circles are examined, some interesting features emerge.

- A minority of the megaliths are stereotypical 'standing' stones - i.e. tall pillars.
- Megaliths which may best be described as blocks or slabs, rather than pillars, and which sit rather than stand upright, occur frequently.
- Certain shapes repeatedly recur, such as pentagons, lozenges/diamonds, triangles and recumbent longstones.
- These shapes are revealed in profile, in a slanting face, or upper surface of the stones.
- The stones appear generally to be unworked.
- The tops of many of the stones appear to be shaped so as to rise to a point.

If the people of Neolithic times chose stones with such characteristics in constructing their stone circles, then these features would seem to offer good templates for megalithic stones occurring in another context – that of potential route waymarks.

A potential megalithic waymark may be described as an unworked stone block, slab or pillar, recumbent, sitting or standing upright. It is typically distinguished from glacial erratics by displaying a triangular, lozenge or pentagonal shape in profile, or on a slanting face or top surface, so as to give a distinct point. It frequently occurs in pairs, and is often located near noticeable natural features such as crags and rock outcrops, stream crossings, waterfalls, and hillocks.

Stone waymarks in Great Langdale

Information is available, then, on the general characteristics of Neolithic routeways; the precedents for marking the way with megaliths; the shapes of stones favoured by the builders of the early – contemporary - Cumbrian stone circles; and the likelihood of a route up Great Langdale from East Yorkshire.

Explorations by the author in Great Langdale have revealed a number of striking megaliths, which seem to display the characteristics of potential waymarks, spaced out up the valley and the slopes below the axe working sites, as described in the following pages. Distinguished by their shapes in profile or the shapes of their upper surfaces, they appear to point in significant directional alignments confirming the actual course of the route up Great Langdale to and from the axe working sites - firstly in the vicinity of the present B 5343 road up the valley; and then up across Stickle Ghyll to the axe working sites. For the first time the likely course of a major route to and from the axe working sites is revealed. Junction routes are also suggested.

This is not the first, or only such way, apparently marked by megaliths, to have been identified in Cumbria by the author. Early explorations revealed likely routes in the east of the county. Further expeditions led to the identification of a number of others elsewhere in Cumbrian Lakeland; these will be described in future publications. Only after much exploration, the realization dawned that the Langdale axe making sites occupied a pivotal position in an unfolding network of apparent Neolithic communication routes. In the light of this, and the known importance of the Neolithic route from the axe stone sources to East Yorkshire, the main way up Great Langdale has been chosen for this first illustration of a Cumbrian way apparently marked by megaliths.

It should be emphasized, to forestall any possible misconception arising, that this work is not a study of ley lines. No reliance is placed on mystical lines of magnetism passing continuously straight over hill and dale, and linking standing stones with hilltops, medieval churches, old crosses, mounds, moats, holy wells and other such features. The focus here is on megaliths. The routes they seem to suggest do not always maintain straight lines, but bend to take account of the natural contours.

Only the most prominent and clearly shaped megaliths are described in this preliminary study. Observant explorers of the route described may identify other likely waymarks. In chapters 2 to 7, a reference number, and a map reference has been applied to each stone in the text. The same reference numbers are applied on the accompanying maps and tables. In the subheading for each stone, the symbol ⇒ is used to indicate the direction pointed by the stone. Measurements of stones are approximate, to the nearest 0.1m. Compass bearings are to the nearest 5°. The map references shown for each stone were recorded using a hand held GPS navigator.

Confidence ratings

The strength of the evidence for identification of the individual megaliths described in the following chapters as Neolithic guidestones, varies from stone to stone. In the tables at the end of each chapter, a star rating has therefore been applied to each stone, to indicate the degree of confidence in the labelling of that stone as a potential waymark. The following simple rating factors have been used in the text. No claim to scientific precision is made; they are intended merely as an approximate guide.

Stones whose rating is limited to one or two stars must be regarded only as possible, tentative markers. It is the stones showing ratings of three or more stars that appear to display the stronger credentials for consideration as likely/more probable guidestones.

Table 1
Star Rating Criteria

Basic star rating	
Recumbent stone, with triangular, lozenge/diamond, pentagonal or longstone shape	*
Slanting or *upright* stone, with shape as above	**
Standing stone	***
A star may be added in respect of each of these features (maximum of two):	
Sharply defined or prominent shape	*
Propped up on another stone	*
Distinctive streaks, cup or ring markings in stone surface	*
Paired or grouped with other possible or probable guidestone(s)	*
A star may be subtracted in respect of each of these features (maximum of two):	
Crudely defined shape	minus *
Too large to be moved	minus *
Part of outcropping rock, not free standing	minus *

Introduction

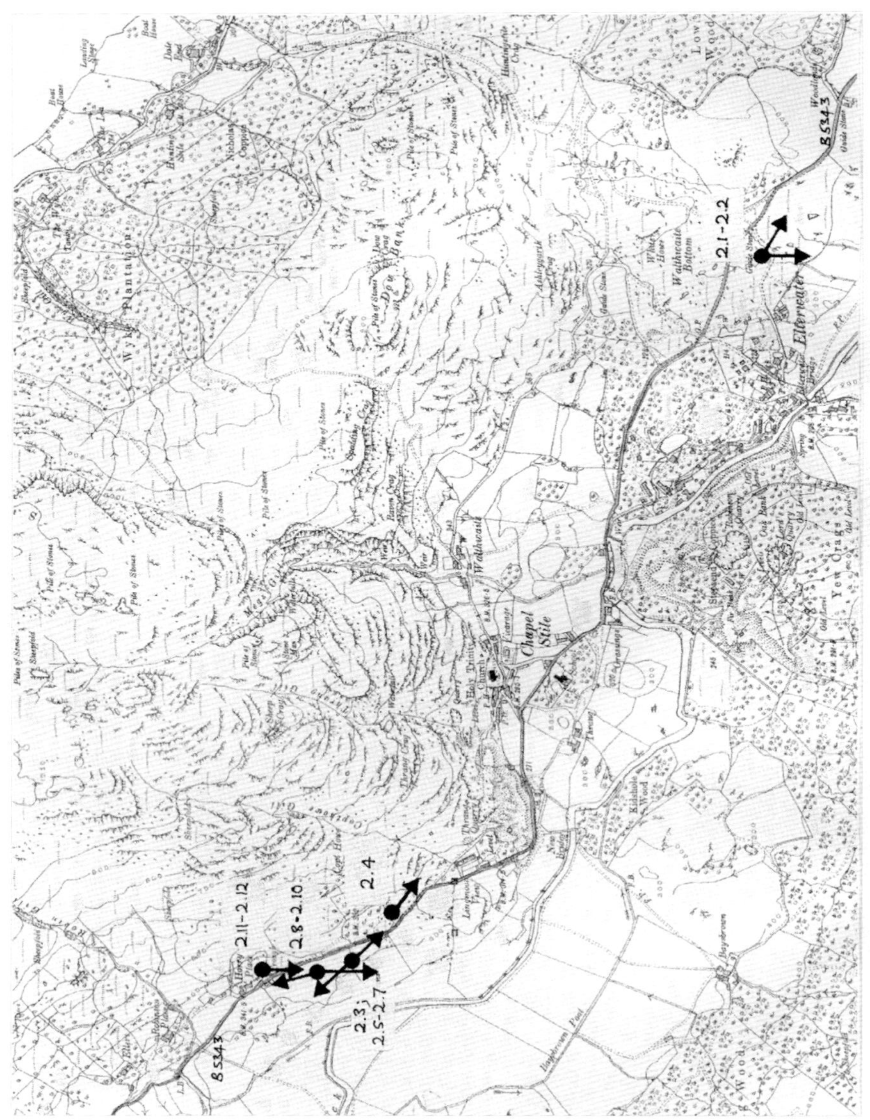

The way past the Rock Art Site, showing locations and alignments of stones 2.1 – 2.12 (Chapter 2)

2 THE WAY PAST THE GREAT LANGDALE ROCK ART SITE

Elterwater Common standing stone

If ancient travellers to the axe factories approached either from the south up Lake Windermere, or from the SE past the head of the lake, and took a low route making their way up beside the River Brathay and past Elterwater, they would arrive at Elterwater Common. The present B road from Skelwith Bridge westward to Great Langdale approaches Elterwater Common at a cattle grid on a brow. The common opens out below, as the Pikes come into view ahead – providing a clear foresight.

2.1 Standing stone slab ⇒ *ESE down the valley*

A little way downhill, a signpost indicates 'Elterwater' at a junction left. On along the Great Langdale road, only about 100m after this road junction, a substantial standing stone may be seen standing at the foot of a hillock back to the left (SW). A slab over 2m tall, it is not recorded on the Ordnance Survey map. It presents a crudely five-sided profile, with a protrusion on the left had side. Viewed from the WNW in front of its smooth, flat vertical face, the line over its wide, blunt pointed top lies ESE down the valley. This is the way past the south side of Loughrigg Tarn to the head of Lake Windermere. If viewed sideways on from the NE, the stone now displays a little three cornered, flat, slanting top with a suggestion of a point in the same direction.

The problem of dating immediately presents itself: there is the possibility that this stone was erected at some date later than the Neolithic Age. Remnants of dry stone walling, and cobbles in the area in front of the standing slab, suggest some construction – possibly a sheep pen or shepherd's hut – beside the stone in recent times. Yet the shape of the stone itself, suggests a Neolithic style, rather than any type likely to have been fashioned in recorded times.

Here, then, at the mouth of the Great Langdale valley, near a gill running down the hillside, stands a major standing stone. The location is important. Outside the exit from the main Great Langdale valley, where possible ways open out in several directions, the standing stone points the way decisively towards the Windermere lakehead. At Loughrigg Tarn, past which it points, a stone axe roughout has been picked up, demonstrating that Neolithic axe stone makers passed by the tarn [1].

Another roughout axe was found not far from Loughrigg Tarn, at High Close [2]. Despite its name, High Close lies at a relatively low elevation of about 150m. The rough out was found near the road leading north from Skelwith Bridge and Loughrigg Tarn to Grasmere through a natural pass at Redbank. The location of this roughout find suggests that the Neolithic stone axe makers also took this way north.

2.2 Recumbent pentagonal stone ⇒ *south to Colwith and Coniston*

In front of the standing slab, a boggy area probably indicates a former tarn, now overgrown. Beyond it to the WNW lies a large recumbent stone. The interesting features

2.1

The pointed top of the Elterwater Common *standing stone* is aligned ESE down the valley towards the head of Lake Windermere. *NY 3311 0487*

2.2

The point of the Elterwater Common *recumbent pentagon* points due south in the direction of a natural way to Coniston. *NY 3307 0491*

of this stone are the distinctly pentagonal shape of its flattish, slightly convex top; and its alignment: the longest point lies due south towards the upper end of Elterwater. This way lies a pass through the fells to Colwith and Coniston, and the way to the Neolithic settlements and axe polishing sites in the Furness peninsula.

To the casual observer this stone may appear unremarkable. However in the context of this study, it is the clear pentagonal shape of this large stone that suggests it as a candidate for a Neolithic guidestone, together with its location beside a former tarn, and its orientation on a cardinal compass point. Even so, it must be regarded as a more tentative example, and is therefore accorded a low points rating.

Three distinct natural stages may be recognized on the way up the Great Langdale valley. A first section sets out NW, then curves westward to the foot of Stickle Ghyll and the slopes leading up to Harrison Stickle. The second part of the valley lies WSW where Great Langdale Beck flows below the south side of Raven Crag and White Crag; from this area a way leads southward over a pass by Side Pike and Blea Tarn. Then a bend in the valley takes it NW again into the third part in Mickleden, and on to the foot of Black Crags at the head of the valley.

In the rest of this chapter some megaliths in the first part of the valley are described. The subsequent two chapters correspond with the other two natural parts of the valley.

Around the Prehistoric Rock Art Site

Along the Great Langdale road through Chapel Stile, the road rises uphill and bends left. Then, after a house called St Anne's the road turns a corner right. A scenic view opens out up the first section of the Great Langdale valley, with Harrison Stickle prominent. From a viewpoint at the beginning of the short stretch of straight road here, a cluster of large rocks may be seen in the pasture below, bisecting a stone wall. These are known in rock climbing circles as the Langdale Boulders. This is the place where the rock art has been discovered.

The lowest rock visible from this viewpoint displays a remarkable side panel of prehistoric rock art; and other cup marked rocks also occur here. Some of the ring markings are thought to date to the Late Neolithic/Early Bronze Age, although the cup marks are probably natural, and additional decorations have been added in the twentieth century [3].

The location is significant. Here the fellsides converge to mark the beginning of the Great Langdale valley proper, with the crags of Thrang Crag (now heavily quarried) rising up on the east. The ancient people chose to mark large rocks at this strategic point with their intriguing ring markings.

2.3

The Langdale Boulders, with the rock art stone on the left. The *slanting diamond block* to its right points north west to Pavey Ark. Harrison Stickle rises high on the distant ridge, with Thorn Crag to its left. *NY 3141 0583*

2.4

The St Anne's *longstone*, on the bank at the edge of the road, is aligned SE down the valley. *NY 3150 0573*

2.3 Upright/slanting diamond block ⇒ *NW up to Pavey Ark*

Before taking a closer look at the site, it may be noticed from this viewpoint up by the corner on the road that, above the lowest large rock, a large, distinctly diamond shaped block lies propped up at a slant on a hillock, at the near edge of the cluster. It points NW up its slanting, uneven top and over its tip, up the valley towards Pavey Ark. In front of Pavey Ark, but invisible from here, lies Stickle Tarn. The characteristics of this stone's slanting diamond top, and its position on a brow near a natural feature (a larger rock outcrop) suggest it as a megalithic guidestone.

2.4 St Anne's recumbent longstone ⇒ *SE down the valley*

On the east side of the road at this corner, a very large, flat sided outcrop of rock towers up almost vertically about 6m. Its cracked face, decorated with a series of cup marks - which appear to have occurred naturally - would have been another landmark for the Neolithic travellers on their way up the valley.

Nearby, back round the corner on the bank on the same side, opposite a house called St Anne's and immediately above the road, a pointed, recumbent, longstone like an ancient spearhead, has a fairly flat top slanting sideways. It points SE down the valley in the direction of Elterwater. Some may dismiss it as a rock fallen here from the crags above. However its position at the corner of the valley, near a prominent natural cup marked rock feature, and its longstone shape with a flat triangular top giving a clear point, suggests it as a possible waymark.

The two cup and ring marked rocks

Access may be gained to the rock art site by a permissive path through a gateway on the left of the road leading down to them. The very large, lowermost rock was prominent on first sight of this cluster from the road. This rock, lying lengthwise north up the valley about 8m long and 5m high, and now encrusted with a top knot of vegetation, is the one which presents the main display of cup and ring markings.

Its NE side faces uphill in the direction of the gate. A number of designs have been pecked on the flattish, nearly upright face, including at least five concentric ring markings, together with a linear design feature and some cup marks. It has recently been shown that the cup marks are natural; and that some ring marks were added during the leisurely doodling of a local bird warden in the 1930s or 1940s [4]! Nevertheless we are left with significant ring markings, and a linear feature, that are thought to date to the Late Neolithic or Early Bronze Age. The linear feature presents a chevron-like shape, considerably extended on one side. Similarities have been noticed with carvings at Glassonby cairn circle in East Cumbria; Temple Wood in Argyll; and the art of the Irish passage graves and megalithic tombs [5].

Above, another very large rock, 7m long, over 5m high, lies up in an easterly alignment through the stone wall. On the upright south face this rock displays just one design of what may be two uncompleted rings; or a deliberately gapped design. Such designs have been noted by Beckensall in Northumberland [6].

Principal *cup and ring* marked rock *NY 3139 0584*

This close up view reveals several ring markings, and also the linear, chevron-style markings (lower right).

2.5

The upper point of this *pentagonal block*, standing over 2m high, points SE - the way followed by the present road round the corner of Thrang Crag. *NY 3140 0583*

2.6

The *triangular stone* 2m high, in the centre of the picture, stands close by the NW side of the second large rock. It again points SE down the valley. *NY 3141 0584*

2.7

A few steps to the north of the rock art cluster, this *recumbent ridged longstone* is again aligned in a similar SE direction down the valley. *NY 3140 0587*

This prehistoric rock art sites carries considerable significance in relation to the present study. Such markings are normally attributed to the people of the Late Neolithic/Early Bronze Age. They indicate that at some stage in this period, people spent time in the vicinity. Moreover such markings have been associated elsewhere – for example in Northumberland – with communication routes [7]. A route along the lower side of the Great Langdale valley is suggested by the location of the rock art site here.

It has already been suggested that one stone seen from the road above appears to have been positioned as a waymark in the vicinity of the rock art site. Further stones apparently performing the function of directional indicators suggest a route past the rock art site that can be dated by association to the Late Neolithic/Early Bronze Age. The more prominent likely stone waymarks include two standing stones, as follows.

2.5 Standing pentagonal block ⇒ SE down the valley

The slanting diamond block on the south edge of the cluster or rocks has already been noted. Nearby down to the west of it, a slim block standing upright, over 2m tall, suggests itself as another possible waymark (although not as sharply defined as some which will be visited). If viewed from the north side it presents a pentagonal profile, with a nearly vertical near end and a sharp upper point and ridge aligned SE past St Anne's, down the valley in the direction of Elterwater – a similar direction to that indicated by the St Anne's pointed longstone.

2.6 Standing triangular slab ⇒ SE down the valley

A ladder stile gives access to the north side of the second cup and ring marked rock bisecting the wall.

Close against the NW side of this large rock, a wide triangular slab stands upright. It is hardly likely to have arrived in this position naturally – some one put it there. It points SE down the valley over its pointed tip, in the same alignment as the previous stone. Here we have an example of a standing pointer slab placed close up to a much larger and more prominent natural rock.

A dozen or so other stones, some substantial, lie in a cluster on this side of the wall. Whilst some of these may possibly have performed a directional function, they are not clearly shaped and will therefore be disregarded.

2.7 Recumbent triangular profile longstone ⇒ SE down the valley

Still on the north side of the wall, a few steps north from the main rock art cluster, beneath the next oak tree, lies a recumbent longstone. Seen end on from the NW, the stone shows a triangular profile. It has a steady ridge interrupted by a little pinnacle in the middle, and rises to its SE end. The line lengthwise up its ridge lies SE yet again down the valley.

2.8 and 2.9

An upright *triangular cup marked block*, with a *lozenge block* perched on top, are both aligned south, at an outcrop opposite the entrance to Copt Howe. *NY 3138 0594*

2.10

An *upright/slanting triangular block* in front of the previous outcrop, leans and points NNW up to the ridge on the side of the valley. *NY 3138 0594*

In this area around the Langdale Boulders, then, we have identified no less than four potential guidestones, three of them pointing down the valley in a 130° - 135° alignment SE towards Elterwater, and two of these being standing stones. The fourth points the opposite way up the valley to the Pikes.

Copt Howe cup marked cluster

Back up on the road, and only a little further along, a cup marked rock – apparently natural - can be seen sitting upright, close by the road on the right. Then, opposite the entrance to Copt Howe, another rock outcrop may be glimpsed in the field over the stone wall on the left. The upright stones on the north side of the outcrop, again display cup marks.

2.8 Upright triangular cupmarked block ⇒ south to Colwith and Coniston
A lower stone with a wide, upright (steeply slanting) triangular face displays about ten cup marks, some nearly 200mm in diameter. However, our interest lies in its alignment: its pointed top ridge is aligned south – in the Coniston direction.

Beside it to the right another upright rounded triangular stone shows about four further cup marks, but no definable shape or point.

2.9 Upright lozenge block ⇒ south to Colwith and Coniston
A stone perched on top of the first, with an upright, crudely rounded lozenge face, is again aligned south over its tip.

Whilst the cup marks may be natural, the shapes and alignments of the stones here are interesting. It would be surprising if the repeated alignments in a southerly direction – a significant route – were purely accidental.

2.10 Upright/slanting triangular block ⇒ up north side of valley
Close in front of these on the north, a block with a flat, slanting, clearly triangular face is aligned a little west of north up over its top point, up to the ridge on the side of the valley in the Blea Crag area. However, relatively low and inconspicuous as it is, this must be regarded as a somewhat tentative marker.

Harry Place Farm stones

A few steps on again, up on the right bank, opposite a gateway on the west side of the road leading down to sheep pens before Harry Place Farm, two separate, sizeable cloven stones appear. Both have cleavages aligned eastwards, in line with one another.

2.11 Streaked lozenge block ⇒ south to Colwith and Coniston
At the foot of the lower cloven stone, immediately above the road, a block with a crudely lozenge profile, but distinguished by the band of white streaked through it, has a blunt point which is aligned due south again.

2.11
This *streaked lozenge block* occurs at the foot of some cloven stones, opposite Harry Place Farm. It points due south along the way taken here by the road. *NY 3138 0600*

2.12
A huge *propped up lozenge stone,* over 3m high, opposite Harry Place Farm, points south at its right side. *NY 3138 0602*

2.12 Harry Place Farm propped-up lozenge ⇒ south to Colwith and Coniston

Only a few more steps further along the fellside above the road, a larger, elongated lozenge shaped stone - at least 3m high - is propped up dramatically against a larger outcrop, to present a steeply slanting face. Its prominent right sided point indicates south yet again – and it leans in this direction.

The emphasis at possible guidestones opposite Copt Howe and Harry Place Farm has been on a southerly alignment, which leads in the direction of a natural way to Coniston Water. No less than four substantial stones point in this direction.

Millbeck Longstones

We now move on along the Great Langdale road, round the side of the valley towards the New Dungeon Ghyll Hotel, and pause at the last brow before the road descends to the Great Langdale car parks, to look at a spaced pair of recumbent longstones near the road.

2.13 Recumbent longstone ⇒ WNW to Stickle Ghyll waterfalls

Just past a barn on the right, and over the brow, a prominent bull nosed longstone lies recumbent uphill in the pasture above the road, aligned slightly north of west. Although not displaying a good point, it has a very significant alignment: this way leads across Stickle Ghyll and up the NE side of Pike Howe, directly to the Harrison Stickle axe working sites. This would provide a direct route from Elterwater Common direction up to the axe stone workings.

2.14 Recumbent longstone ⇒ WSW up the valley

Another longstone lies a little nearer to the road beside a dry stream bed, its flattish face slanting sideways. This one is aligned (with a better side point) SW up the valley.

To modern eyes these stones may at first appear unremarkable. But this spaced pair of longstones, situated near a gill, both with their faces angled so as to be seen from below, appear to mark a fork in the routes, which could have been recognised and understood by Neolithic travellers.

2.13
At Millbeck, a prominent recumbent longstone over 3m long, is aligned WNW towards Stickle Ghyll falls.
NY 2978 0559

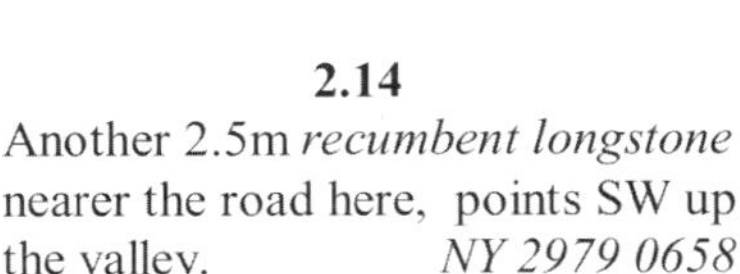

2.14
Another 2.5m *recumbent longstone* nearer the road here, points SW up the valley. *NY 2979 0658*

Table 2a

Guidestones, and directions pointed in Chapter 2

Guide stone no.	Type	Align-ment	Situation	Guide stone rating
⇒	**Pointers to Windermere**			
2.1	Standing stone slab	120°	foot of hillock by gill	***
2.4	Recumbent longstone	130°	low corner of fellside	*
2.5	Standing pentagonal block	135°	at rock art site	***
2.6	Standing triangular slab	135°	at rock art site	****
2.7	Recumbent triangular profile longstone	130°	at rock art site	**
⇒	**Pointers to Coniston**			
2.2	Recumbent pentagonal stone	180°	by overgrown tarn	*
2.8	Upright triangular block	180°	foot of outcrop near rock art site	**
2.9	Upright lozenge block	180°	on outcrop near rock art site	***
2.11	Upright lozenge block	180°	foot of large cloven stones	**
2.12	Standing lozenge slab	180°	low fell side	***
⇒	**Pointers to the Pikes**			
2.3	Upright/slanting diamond block	315°	up hillock at rock art site	****
2.10	Upright/slanting triangular block	345°	foot of outcrop near rock art site	**
2.13	Recumbent bull nosed longstone	290°	low fell near beck	**
⇒	**Pointer up the valley**			
2.14	Recumbent pointed longstone	245°	low fell near beck	**

Table 2b

Stone types and features – Chapter 2

Stone no.	Type	Size	Features	Map ref. (NY)
▯	**Standing stones**			
2.1	Standing stone slab	2.2m H	prominent; top point	3311 0487
2.5	Standing pentagonal block	2.1m H	1 of 4 at rock art site	3140 0583
2.6	Standing triangular slab	2.0m H	1 of 4 at rock art site	3141 0584
△	**Triangular stones**			
2.6	Standing triangular slab	*see*	*standing stones above*	3141 0584
2.7	Recumbent triangular longstone	1.7m L	1 of 4 at rock art site	3140 0587
2.8	Upright triangular cup marked block	1.3m H	cup marked; grouped with 2.9, 2.10	3138 0594
2.10	Upright/slanting triangular block	1.1m H	grouped with 2.8, 2.9	3138 0594
◇	**Lozenge/diamond stones**			
2.3	Upright/slanting diamond block	2.3m H	prominent; 1 of 4 at rock art site	3141 0583
2.9	Upright lozenge block	1.3m H	perched on 2.8	3138 0594
2.11	Upright lozenge block	1.4m H	streaked	3138 0600
2.12	Propped upright lozenge slab	3m+ H	propped up; very large	3138 0602
⬠	**Pentagonal stones**			
2.2	Recumbent pentagonal stone	2.5m L		3307 0491
2.5	Standing pentagonal block	*see*	*standing stones above*	3140 0583
▭	**Longstones**			
2.4	Recumbent spearhead style longstone	2.7m L	near pitted rock face	3150 0573
2.7	Recumbent triangular longstone	*see*	*triang. stones above*	3140 0587
2.13	Recumbent bullnosed longstone	3.4m L	paired with 2.14	2978 0559
2.14	Recumbent pointed longstone	2.5m L	paired with 2.13	2979 0658

Summary: The way past the Great Langdale Rock Art Site

Finds of artefacts, and the rock art site

It has been seen that the volume of Group VI stone axes discovered in the East Yorkshire area indicates that there must have been important cross country links ESE in that direction from the axe working sites. This implies a route down Great Langdale. The question was raised as to whether the axe makers took a high route along the ridge running alongside the valley on the NE side, or a lower route along the valley itself.

The evidence of the three relevant artefactual finds in or near this first part of the valley tends to indicate a route or routes along the valley side. One axe roughout has been picked up by Loughrigg Tarn, low down in the valley, showing that the Neolithic people came by here. Another similar find – at High Close – lies in a low pass through the ridge to Grasmere. Not far up the valley beyond Harry Place Farm, Robin Gill runs down the fellside to Great Langdale Beck. A broken stone chisel was found by this gill, apparently near a house low down the fellside in the vicinity of the gill. No Neolithic sites or finds of artefacts have been reported along the ridge, so far as the author is aware.

The rock art site on the lower valley side provides further evidence of the presence of people there at some time in the Late Neolithic/Early Bronze Age, although it remains to be certainly established that the site was contemporary with axe production at the Great Langdale axe workings.

Directions indicated (Table 2a)

Some first signs of likely megalithic markers on a route along Great Langdale have been identified.

Three particular alignments are repeatedly displayed by the stones:
- down the valley towards the head of Windermere;
- down the valley bearing south towards the head of Coniston; and
- up to the Pikes.

A pointer at Millbeck also indicates the continuing way up the valley.

ESE towards Windermere

The megaliths at the rock art site, and Elterwater Common, lie in an area where the natural confines of the Great Langdale valley sides give way to more ambiguous terrain offering different options for onward travel. In this environment, no less than five stones have been identified (including three with a three star rating or higher), which indicate the ESE way out of the valley towards Elterwater and/or the head of Lake Windermere (stones 2.1, 2.4, 2.5, 2.6, 2.7). Stones in the vicinity of the rock art site repeatedly show this alignment. All three of the standing stones are aligned this way.

South towards Coniston
Five further stones, four of them opposite the Copt Howe entrance and Harry Place Farm, are aligned in a direction which leads southwards towards Little Langdale and Coniston, suggesting an important route in this direction (2.2, 2.8, 2.9, 2.11, 2.12). However, the first of these are more tentative waymarks. The most striking indicator is the massive propped up lozenge near Harry Place Farm.

Up to the axe working sites
Three stones point different ways up towards the Pikes (2.3, 2.10, 2.13). The first and strongest one – the prominent slanting diamond block at the rock art site - points in the Pavey Ark/Stickle Tarn direction. Another more tentative stone at the Copt Howe cup marked stones points up to the ridge in the Blea Crag area. One prominent longstone at Millbeck possibly suggests the way up via the Stickle Ghyll waterfalls.

Up the valley
One longstone at Millbeck suggests the continuing way up the valley (2.14).

Stone types and groups (Table 2b)

The megaliths which have been identified as potential guidestones, show characteristics similar to those found in stone circles of the period. Three *standing* stones have been identified. The standing stone slab on Elterwater Common has been the most outstanding specimen (2.1). A standing pentagonal block and a standing triangular slab have also occurred in close association with the rock art site (2.5 and 2.6). Other upright, slanting and recumbent stones, comparable to those found in stone circles, have occurred.

This chapter has provided an introduction to four main shapes which repeatedly recur in potential guidestones: triangular, lozenge/diamond, pentagonal and longstone shapes, as follows.

The *triangular* shape has appeared four times. Most notable is the standing triangular stone slab close up beside the second largest of the Langdale Boulders (2.6). Other examples are the lower of the upright cup marked stones opposite Copt Howe entrance (2.8); and the slanting stone north below these cup marked stones (2.10). The shape appears again in the profile of a longstone (2.7).

The *lozenge* or *diamond* shape is prominently represented in the slanting diamond block at the south side of the Langdale Boulders (2.3). There is also an upright, lozenge faced block opposite Copt Howe (2.9), and the shape appears again in the slanting surface of the smaller stone below the Harry Place Farm cloven stones (2.11). This stone is further distinguished by a vein of quartz running through it. The huge propped-up lozenge – almost a standing stone - nearer to Harry Place Farm (2.12), provides a further conspicuous example.

The *pentagonal* shape is represented in the top of the recumbent stone on Elterwater Common (2.2); and in the profile of a standing stone to the SE of the rock art site (2.5).

Four substantial recumbent *longstones* have been identified. One resembling a spearhead lies at St Anne's (2.4), and another with a triangular profile and sharp ridge, sits north of the main Langdale Boulders (2.7). A further pair of substantial specimens have appeared at Millbeck (2.13 & 2.14). The *pairing* of stones, seen first in this chapter at Millbeck, will be encountered a number of times in later chapters.

Locations

The situation of these and other potential waymark stones on the lower slopes of the fellside, but above the valley floor, will be a recurring feature in these pages. So, too, will be the positioning of stones near a gill, and at the side of a hillock.

The cluster around the rock art site occurs where the hillside protrudes at a corner into the valley. One prominent, naturally occurring, cup marked rock face draws attention to a likely stone waymark nearby. At the Langdale Boulders, large rocks – which presumably occur naturally – are used to draw attention to other stones, apparently directional, associated with them. The substantial cloven stones up the fellside near Harry Place Farm appear again to draw attention to a likely guidestone at their foot.

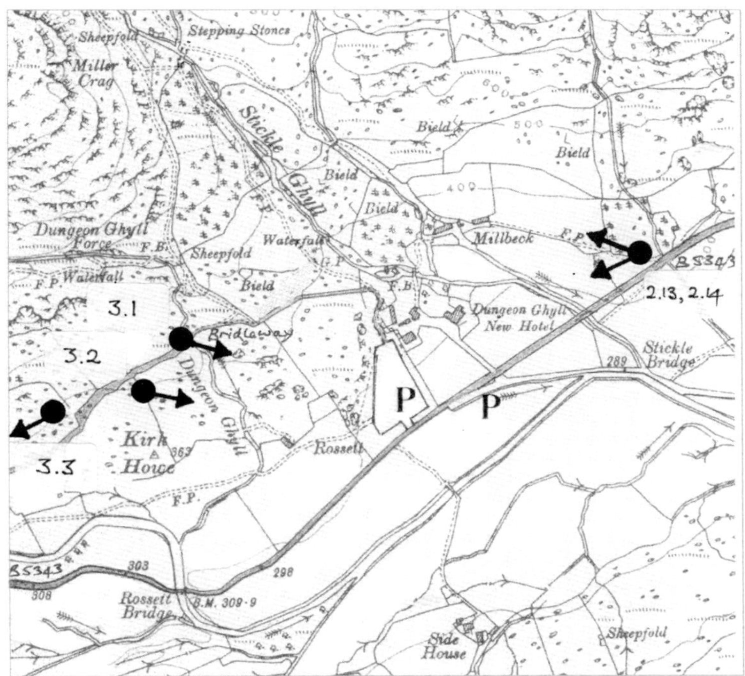

The area around the New Dungeon Ghyll Hotel and National Trust car parks, showing stones 2.13 and 2.14 (Chapter 2), and stones 3.1 to 3.3 (Chapter 3)

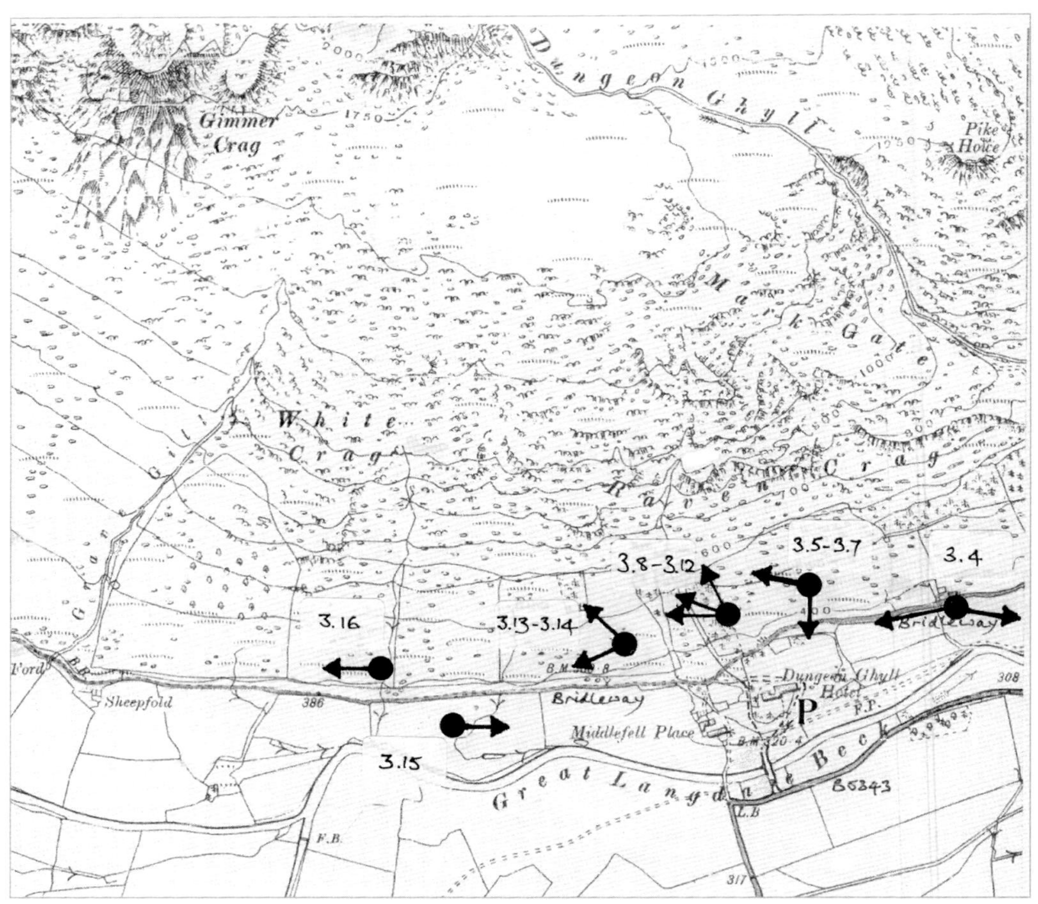

The bridleway past Raven Crag, showing locations and alignments of stones 3.4 to 3.16 (Chapter 3)

3 THE BRIDLEWAY PAST RAVEN CRAG

One route suggested by the Millbeck longstones lies up towards the axe working sites, and the other continues along the valley. The valley route will first be explored in this and the next chapter, and the way up to the axe working sites in chapters 5, 6 and 7.

We have now reached the point where the Great Langdale valley has turned to take a WSW course past Raven Crag and White Crag on the north side.

Dungeon Ghyll crossing

From the brow at Millbeck, the Great Langdale road descends to the valley bottom. Signs of megalithic markers along in the vicinity of the road peter out here, which is not surprising, given the preference of Neolithic people for trackways off the valley floor. However, from the second Great Langdale National Trust Car Park, on the right of the road NW of New Dungeon Ghyll Hotel, a bridleway picks up the way along the lower slope of the hillside, up the valley. This chapter continues with a description of some megalithic specimens visible along this track. The bridleway may be reached by a footpath from the car park.

3.1 Dungeon Ghyll standing triangular stump ⇒ ESE down the valley

Immediately before this track crosses Dungeon Ghyll on a footbridge, a stone stump stands upright, over 1m high, on the left of the track. Other possible guidestones may be picked out on the banks of the gill below the bridge.

If viewed from beyond on the west side, the stone shows its best profile. A steeply slanting face, very slightly concave, and with a slightly curved triangular profile, rises to a point ESE. The curvature mimics the way cutting off a corner, back down the SW side of the bending Great Langdale valley towards the rock art site.

Evidence accumulated from ways across other watercourses suggests that this is a typical stream crossing marker, positioned so that, on an approach to the stream, it was visible pointing the way ahead beyond on the far side.

Kirk Howe

3.2 Upright/slanting lozenge block ⇒ ESE down the valley

A little way on along the track, in a meadow below the stone wall on the north side of Kirk Howe, a large block perches prominently on a brow. It displays a slanting flat back with a striking lozenge shape, and points ESE over its upper tip down the valley again. This is a fine specimen, comparable to the slanting diamond block pointing up the valley at the Langdale Boulders (stone 2.3).

3.1

This *standing triangular stump* beside the footbridge across Dungeon Ghyll, reveals a concave face slanting up to a point aligned ESE down the valley. *NY 2917 0647*

3.2

A large, prominent *upright/slanting lozenge block*, perched on a brow near Kirk Howe, again points the way ESE down the valley. *NY 2910 0639*

3.3 Upright triangular topped block ⇒ *WSW up the valley*
Next along the track, a huge block comes into view, lying up the side of a hillock off to the right of the track. Its wide triangular top slopes sideways; the upper tip points WSW, which leads along the hillside up the valley ahead.

Several substantial stones on the top of the hillock above, displaying the familiar triangular, lozenge and pentagonal shapes, point in a direction slightly east of north, strongly suggesting a route crossing the valley this way from the Blea Tarn direction, and leading on up Pike Howe round the end of Raven Crag. However, detailed description of these must await a future publication.

Wayside barn

3.4 Slanting lozenge block ⇒ *up the valley / down the valley*
Beside the track opposite a small barn, a block of stone approached from the east, presents an uneven, slanting back in a lozenge shape rising to a point aligned WSW up along the bridleway. The alignment is slightly ambiguous: if maintained, it leads in the middle distance across the valley to the foot of a hill called The Band, up which a path lies westward to Eskdale, via the pass at Three Tarns.

Then from beyond on the west side, the stone reveals an upright leaf arrowhead profile, pointing ESE down the valley. This could be an example of a two-way guidestone.

Below Raven Crag

A short diversion uphill off the track is required, to see the next stones.

3.5 Upright lozenge block ⇒ *south to Redacre Gill*
In front of a fenced larch wood uphill off the track, two smaller stones prop up a large block. It has a flattish, almost vertical rounded lozenge style face, and a rounded top, with the suggestion of a southward point at the left hand side. If a viewpoint is taken from the north behind, this stone now presents an upright lozenge profile confirming the southward alignment. It points due south over its tip – across the valley towards Redacre Gill, perhaps leading on over Wrynose Fell to Wrynose Pass. Beside Redacre Gill in this direction, ancient cairns have been identified.

3.6 Slanting longstone ⇒ *WNW to Gimmer Crag*
Behind, over the fence, a longstone leans propped up at a slant behind a larger rock, its upper pointed end aligned slightly north of west. This could be an important indicator. It leads towards the start of the Gimmer Crag path, above Middle Fell Farm, towards which further waymarks will be identified shortly. This path gives access to the Thorn Crag pass to Loft Crag and Pike o' Stickle. It could also indicate the need to start climbing the fellside, proceeding past the foot of White Crag, for easy access to the Pike o' Stickle south scree and buttress axe working sites from an approach diagonally up Langdale Fell.

3.3

Up the side of a hillock off to the right of the path sits this substantial *triangular topped block* 4m high, pointing WSW up the valley. *NY 2899 0635*

3.4

A *slanting lozenge block* sits opposite a small barn; seen from the east side, its lozenge back points WSW along the path. *NY 2880 0624*

3.5
Two smaller stones prop up this large *lozenge block*, which points south out across the valley. *NY 2871 0629*

3.6 and **3.7**
A *longstone* behind a huge, pentagon topped block, slants up in a line WNW, which leads diagonally up the fellside. *NY 2871 0629*

3.7 Slanting pentagon topped block ⇒ *WNW to Gimmer Crag*

The huge pentagonal topped rock beyond it also slants up to a point in the same direction, although it is too large to have been manhandled by the Neolithic people. The larger rock appears to have been used to draw attention to the smaller waymark.

The Three Scots Pines

Along the track a little further, approaching a gate above Old Dungeon Ghyll Hotel, some striking stones are located around three Scots Pines on a hillock off to the right above the track. The steep rock faces of Raven Crag tower up above – now a favoured rock climbing site, which would have been a prominent natural feature in ancient times.

3.8 Standing pentagonal stone ⇒ *west up the valley*

On the eastern side of the brow an impressive stone block stands almost vertical. It displays a flat pentagonal face, jagged on one edge, rising to an upper point. The line over its pointed tip lies due west along the side of the hill up the valley.

This standing stone – not recorded on the Ordnance Survey maps – exemplifies some of the key characteristics of potential waymark megaliths. It presents a sharp pentagonal profile. It points due west along the hillside – the way up the valley. It is located conspicuously on the brow of a hillock, below the natural feature of Raven Crag.

3.9 Recumbent lozenge topped block ⇒ *west up the valley*

Between the two upper pine trees lies a recumbent stone supported on cobbles. Although less striking, it has a flat, crudely lozenge top, slanting sideways and also pointing west up the valley, when seen from an eastern approach.

3.10 Recumbent lozenge topped block ⇒ *NNW to Thorn Crag path*

Half a dozen paces west from the last, a recumbent stone has a fairly flat, kite/lozenge shaped top, slanting gently up to a point NNW – a direction which leads up via the Gimmer Crag path to the Thorn Crag pass – a way towards Loft Crag, Harrison Combe and Pike o' Stickle axe factories.

3.11 Upright/slanting pentagonal block ⇒ *NNW up the crags*

Through on the west side of the pines, another impressive stone - the largest block here at over 3m high - presents a striking pentagonal face, slanting up to a point aligned slightly west of north up to a gully at the end of Raven Crag above, when seen broadside on from the south side below.

Wainwright, in his volume on the central fells, says that he climbed this gully [1]. It again provides access to the Thorn Crag path leading to Pike o' Stickle above. If Wainwright could find his way up here, the fit young axe workers of Neolithic times would surely have been able to do the same.

3.8

An impressive *pentagonal standing stone*, 2m high, points due west up the valley at the three Scots Pines. *NY 2853 0623*

3.9

A *lozenge topped recumbent block* nearby, also points west up the valley. Stones 3.11 and 3.12 may be seen to the left ahead. *NY 2852 0622*

3.10

Another *recumbent lozenge topped block* points NW towards the Thorn Crag path. *NY 2851 0622*

3.11
A very large stone displays a striking *pentagonal face,* slanting upward towards Raven Crag NNW above.
NY 2850 0622

3.11 and **3.12**
The same block, seen sideways on from the SE, reveals a relatively smaller *pentagonal style stone* (still 1.7m high) lodged upright at its top end, pointing WNW. *NY 2850 0622*

However, they are more likely to have avoided the high, steep crags here and opted for an easier route round to the east or west of the crags.

3.12 Upright pentagonal stone ⇒ *WNW up the valley*

If the same block is viewed from the SE, a smaller pentagonal style stone with a sharp upper point is revealed lodged up against its top end. Seen from this side, both stones in the pair indicate a WNW direction up the valley. This repeats the indication given by the slanting longstone (3.6 above) of the need to aim gently up the fellside past the foot of White Crag towards the Pike o' Stickle south scree.

Stones NW/west above Middle Fell Farm

3.13 Slanting triangular block ⇒ *NNW to Gimmer Crag path*

Now the bridleway will be followed on through the gate above Old Dungeon Ghyll Hotel westward towards Mickleden. After the turning down to Old Dungeon Ghyll Hotel, the track passes a ladder stile a little way above, taking a junction path into a little larch wood above the track. A spaced pair of substantial blocks then appear in the pasture above the stone wall. Viewed from the bank above the track, the upper, more prominent block shows an elongated triangular shape, pointing NNW over its upper tip up the crags. Viewed from the WSW further along the track, its upright side suggests a lozenge on its side, also pointing uphill this way.

This large, striking megalith marks a significant route. A path still leads this way to Gimmer Crag and the pass by Thorn Crag, giving access to the axe chipping sites at Loft Crag and Pike o' Stickle. A number of further likely guidestones occur up the path to confirm this route.

3.14 Triangular block ⇒ *West up the valley / WSW to Oxendale*

The other block at first appears to have a crudely rounded triangular top slanting sideways, its uplifted point aligned westward up the valley. However, if a detour is made up the path over the ladder stile into the larch wood, and the stone is then viewed from a standpoint higher up through the wood, it reveals a triangular profile and a back slanting up to a point aligned WSW up Oxendale.

3.15 Upright triangular block ⇒ *east down the valley*

Back along below the bridleway, past a gill running down the second field on the left below, is located a stepped block with a flat top slanting gently. Seen first from above north on the track, the top appears to have a resemblance to a leaf arrowhead, its upper point indicating a SE direction across towards Blea Tarn - the way to Little Langdale and the south.

However, if viewed from further west along the track, the stone now takes on the sharp profile of an upright triangle, apparently indicating the way east down the valley. This is likely to have been the primary way indicated by what may be a two-way marker.

3.13 and **3.14**

Two large *slanting triangular topped blocks* are conspicuous NW above Middle Fell Farm. The nearest stone (3.14) points west across to Oxendale; the other NW up the Gimmer Crag path. *NY 2838 0616 and NY 2839 0615*

3.15

An *upright triangular block* below the bridleway is aligned east down the valley. *NY 2812 0610*

3.16 Upright, dented diamond sided block ⇒ *west up the valley*

Past an outcrop of rock on the upper side of the track, and west of a dividing wall separating the meadows above, another stone lies by a gill. This large block, beside a hawthorn tree, has a 'dented' flat diamond face which slants sideways and points west again along the valley.

3.16
A 'dented' diamond sided block sits to the left of a hawthorn tree, its long point aligned west up the valley. *NY 2806 0615*

Summary: The Bridleway past Raven Crag

Directions indicated (Table 3a)

No prehistoric sites, or finds of relevant artefacts of the period have yet been reported in this part of the valley. What has emerged is:

- a striking number of possible megalithic waymarks, including two more standing stones, pointing the way up and down the valley, spaced out at frequent intervals along the lower slope of the hillside;
- increased signs of guidestones up the fellsides to the axe working sites.

Up the valley

Megalithic waymarks continue to point the apparent direction of a way up and down the valley. It is remarkable how many of the stones - no less than six - now point the way up the valley (3.3, 3.4, 3.8, 3.9, 3.14, 3.16). They include a 5 star standing pentagonal stone at the three Scots Pines, and a 3 star diamond sided block; together with other more tentative markers. These stones are indicative of a way in this direction, along the low fellside. This would give access to the Pike o' Stickle axe 'factory' from the SE, and also continuing routes NW and north over the passes at the head of the valley.

Down the valley

Four stones have been identified which mark the way down the valley (3.1, 3.2, 3.4, 3.15). Three of these have 3 star ratings or higher. They include two striking examples: a standing stone – the Dungeon Ghyll stump; and the prominent Kirk Howe slanting lozenge, positioned strategically on a brow, providing a particularly emphatic directional indication down the valley, up over the point of its slanting back. A slanting lozenge block, and an upright triangular block past Middle Fell Farm, also point this way.

Up to the axe working sites from the ESE

Now, closer to the high axe chipping sites, further ways up to them from the valley are indicated. The strong inference from the megalithic markers is that more than one way was established up to the axe stone sources.

- The large slanting triangular block NW of Middle Fell Farm points emphatically to the start of the Gimmer Crag path up to the Pikes (3.13). A recumbent lozenge at the three Scots Pines also marks this way (3.10). If this path is followed up through the crags, a number of further potential waymarks may be identified confirming this route (which will have to await description in a future publication).

- The slanting long block (3 star) and pentagon topped block below Raven Crag could, similarly, be seen as pointing up in the direction of the start of the Gimmer Crag path (3.6 & 3.7). These stones could also be interpreted as marking a gentle diagonal ascent past this path up the hillside, passing below White Crag and up the side of Langdale Fell to the Pike o' Stickle south scree and buttresses. This line is reinforced by the large upright/slanting pentagon and baby companion at the three Scots Pines (3.11 and 3.12) – both fairly strong candidates for guidestones.

Table 3a

Guidestones, and directions pointed in Chapter 3

Guide stone no.	Type	Aign-ment	Situation	Guide stone rating
⇒	**Pointers down the valley**			
3.1	Standing triangular stump	105°	on bank of D. Ghyll by crossing	****
3.2	Slanting lozenge block	100°	on a brow	****
3.4	Slanting lozenge block	100°	low fellside	**
3.15	Upright triangular block	90°	fell foot near gill	***
⇒	**Pointers up the valley**			
3.3	Upright triangular topped block	245°	on side of hillock	**
3.4	Slanting lozenge block	255°	low fellside	**
3.8	Standing pentagonal stone	270°	on brow of hillock	*****
3.9	Recumbent lozenge topped block	270°	on hillock	**
3.14	Slanting triangular block	270°	low fell side	**
3.16	Upright diamond sided block	270°	by a gill	***
⇒	**Pointers up Raven Crag**			
3.10	Recumbent lozenge topped block	330°	on hillock	**
3.13	Slanting triangular block	330°	low fellside	***
⇒	**Pointers up to Pike o' Stickle**			
3.6	Slanting long stone	280°	low fellside	***
3.7	Slanting pentagon topped block	280°	low fellside	**
3.11	Upright/slanting pentagonal stone	290°	low fellside	****
3.12	Upright pentagonal stone	290°	low fellside	***
⇒	**Pointers to Wrynose Pass**			
3.5	Upright lozenge block	180°	low fellside	***
3.14	Slanting triangular block	245°	low fellside	**

South to Redacre Gill and Wrynose Pass / WSW to Oxendale
One stone suggests a new direction - a southward route to Redacre Gill, giving access to Wrynose Pass (3.5). Two stones may be oriented towards Oxendale (3.4, 3.14), which could again lead to a way to Wrynose Pass: although these are both tentative markers.

Stone types and groups (Table 3b)
Two *standing stones* have occurred in this section - the striking standing stone pentagon near the three Scots Pines (3.8); and the standing stump on the bank of Dungeon Ghyll.

A *triangular* shape has occurred four times. A huge triangular backed block has been seen NW of Kirk Howe (3.3). The very large slanting block pointing the way up to Gimmer Crag displays a triangular top (3.13); as does the spaced paired block in the same pasture (3.14). A further upright triangular block stands west of Middle Fell Farm (3.15).

The *lozenge* or *diamond* shape appears no less than seven times – at the prominent Kirk Howe slanting lozenge (3.2), the wayside barn stone, (3.4) the Raven Crag upright block (3.5), in two recumbent stones at the Scots Pines (3.9 and 3.10); in the side of the prominent uphill pointer block NW of Middle Fell Farm (3.13), and the sideways dented diamond block further NW (3.16).

Four *pentagonal* examples have been identified, three of them emphatic ones: the huge stone in front of the Raven Crag longstone (3.7); the three Scots Pines standing stone (3.8); and the large three Scots Pines upright/slanting stone (3.11). The smaller stone lodged up against the last provides a fourth example (3.12). A *longstone* propped up at a slant has occurred below Raven Crag (3.6).

The *pairing* of stones has been noted three times. Of particular interest in this section of the route, examples of large stones paired closely with relatively small ones have occurred twice. One example is the slanting longstone with its huge companion below Raven Crag (3.6 & 3.7); another is the large slanting pentagon at the three Scots Pines with its small partner (3.11 & 3.12). Such pairs might be classified as 'mother and baby' pairs. A third, more evenly matched, spaced pairing occurs in the large spaced pair NW of Middle Fell Farm (3.13 & 3.14). A group cluster of at least five potential waymarks occurs below Raven Crag at the three Scots Pines.

Locations
The positioning of likely waymarks along the lower slopes of the hillside continues. Likely waymarks occur in a cluster at the three Scots Pines, below the natural feature of Raven Crag, above Old Dungeon Ghyll Hotel. The siting of stones by a stream crossing recurs in this part of the exploration with the Dungeon Ghyll stump; and with stones sited by gills west of Middle Fell Farm. More examples have occurred of the siting of stones at prominent brows and hillocks – at Kirk Howe, and at the three Scots Pines.

Table 3b

Stone types and features – Chapter 3

Stone no.	Type	Size	Features	Map ref. (NY)
	Standing stones			
3.1	Standing triangular stump	1.1m H	grouped with other stones downstream	2917 0647
3.8	Standing pentagonal stone	2.2m H	grouped with 3.9, 3.10, 3.11, 3.12	2853 0623
	Triangular stones			
3.1	Standing triangular stump		*see standing stones above*	
3.3	Upright triangular topped block	4m H	large and prominent	2899 0635
3.13	Slanting triangular topped block	tbc	lozenge sided; paired with 3.14	2838 0616
3.14	Slanting triangular block	tbc	paired with 3.13	2839 0615
3.15	Upright triangular block	tbc	strong triangular profile	2812 0610
	Lozenge / diamond stones			
3.2	Slanting lozenge block		large and prominent	2910 0639
3.4	Slanting lozenge block	1.5m H		2880 0624
3.5	Upright lozenge block	3.2m H	propped up	2871 0629
3.9	Recumbent lozenge topped block	1.5m L	grouped with 3.8, 3.10, 3.11, 3.12	2852 0622
3.10	Recumbent lozenge topped block	1.5m L	grouped with 3.8, 3.9, 3.11, 3.12	2851 0622
3.13	Upright lozenge sided block		*see triangular stones above*	
3.16	Upright diamond sided block	tbc	dented face	2806 0615
	Pentagonal stones			
3.7	Slanting pentagon topped block	c6m L	very large; paired with 3.6	2871 0629
3.8	Standing pentagonal stone		*see standing stones above*	
3.11	Upright/slanting pentagon stone	3.2m H	prominent; paired with 3.12	2850 0622
3.12	Upright pentagonal stone	1.7m H	small; paired close up to 3.11	2850 0622
	Longstones			
3.6	Slanting long block	2m L	paired with 3.7	2871 0629

The Bridleway past Raven Crag

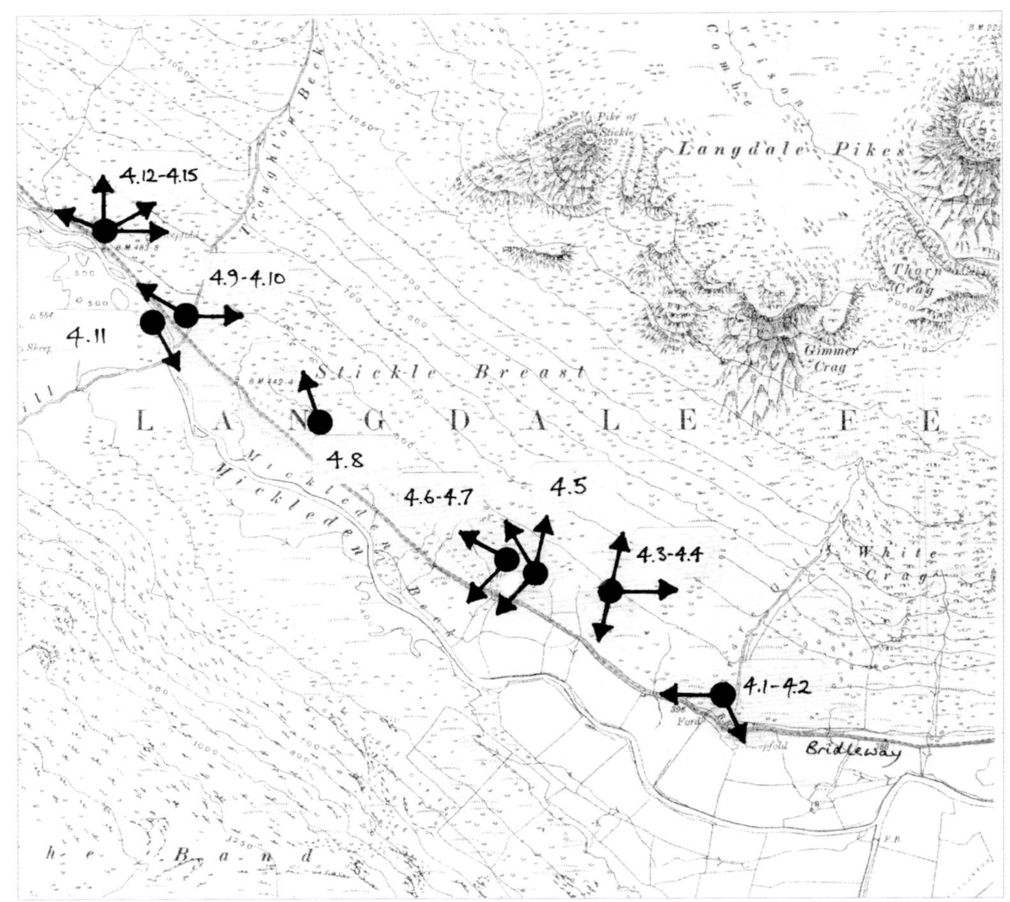

The Mickleden way, showing the locations and alignments of stones 4.1 – 4.15 (Chapter 4)

4 THE MICKLEDEN WAY

Grave Gill

The bridleway passes through two gates by sheepfolds, and bends round the foot of the fellside - a significant natural feature. The stone wall gives way to the open slope of Langdale Fell on the right. Here the top section of Great Langdale opens up, lying NW again like the first part of the valley. The most productive axe stone source – Pike o' Stickle – looks down on the valley from the NE above.

4.1 Recumbent, slanting pentagon topped block ⇒ SSE to Blea Tarn

Soon Grave Gill runs downhill on the right. Not far up the gill on the east side, a large block is prominent. It presents a crudely pentagonal shaped flattish top, slanting sideways and down to a blunt point over the valley SE, towards Blea Tarn and Little Langdale. The upper blunt end of the top is aligned towards Pike o' Stickle - now visible up on the right. However, as this end is not pointed, and as likely guidestones are typically situated on the far side of an approach to a stream crossing, the downward point may be taken as the directional indicator.

4.2 Recumbent lozenge topped block ⇒ west across Mickleden Beck

Paired with it close by above on the bank of the beck, a much smaller block has a flattish lozenge shaped top, slanting gently downwards to a west point. Here we have another mother and baby pair. The alignment is interesting. With the turn in the hillside, the westerly alignment of the small stone no longer points up the valley, but across it. In this direction lies the modern footbridge across Mickleden Beck, an ancient cairnfield, and further off the high hillside of Earing Crag, and the way across to other axe chipping sites in the direction of Sca Fell.

4.1 and **4.2**

This recumbent slanting pentagon and baby lozenge topped companion sit on the edge of Grave Gill. The larger stone points SE towards Blea Tarn; and the smaller one west across the valley. *NY 2764 0618*

4.3
An upright *triangular block,* standing 2m high, points SSW across The Band towards Pike o' Blisco. *NY 2750 0636*

4.4
This large *slanting triangular sided block,* 3m long, points east down the valley. *NY 2750 0637*

Lower Langdale Fell

From here, over open ground uphill above the bridleway, along the lower slope of Langdale Fell, a series of stones may be detected leading away from the stream, in a NW direction along the lower hillside. No present day footpath follows the way described; however, the ground is easily traversed, provided that the season of high summer is avoided, when the encroaching bracken hampers progress and makes the stones less easy to detect.

4.3 Upright triangular block ⇒ NNE to Gimmer Crag/SSW to The Band

After several crudely shaped markers spaced out this way, a larger pair of blocks stands out prominently ahead. On a closer view the first - lower - one proves to be a fine specimen of a large triangular standing block. If viewed from in front of its upright flat face, which leans slightly back from vertical, the point gives a direction a touch east of north up to Gimmer Crag on the ridge above. However, when seen from its other (north) side, the line up its ridge to the point indicates slightly west of south across the foot of The Band – the way to Oxendale and Wrynose Pass.

4.4 Slanting, triangular sided block ⇒ East down the valley/WNW to Rossett Hause

The other, larger stone in the pair sits 20 paces above to the north, encrusted with dark lichen. It displays a triangular shaped top which slants steeply sideways and points due east along the hillside – a strong down valley indicator. If now viewed from the north above, it can be seen to have a ridge slanting up to a bull nosed point, aligned in a 290° WNW direction up towards Rossett Gill at the head of the valley. This would of course be the profile seen by axe stone workers higher up the fellside above.

Pike o' Stickle pentagon

4.5 Standing pentagonal block ⇒ to Stake Pass/Pike o' Stickle/The Band

After about 100 paces further NW, the fellside drops down to the valley floor. A very substantial, prominent standing block comes into view between two gills towards the bridleway.

From this SSE approach the standing block displays a flat upper face, with a crack down the middle, slanting steeply up to a tip aligned 330° NNW towards Mart Crag. Beyond in this direction lies Stake Pass and the way north down Langstrath and Borrowdale.

However, when viewed broadside on from the SSW below, it now presents an impressive upright pentagonal profile reminiscent of some stones at the great Avebury stone circle. It points 10° just east of north, up to the ridge of the Pikes above. Its sharp top ridge rises up this way. Could this stone have been erected in symbolic dedication to the crags above, so richly productive of stone for axes? When viewed from the other side NE above, the line across the tip lies 220° SW across to the hillside of The Band opposite – the way to Wrynose Pass; and the upright face on this side leans a little forward this way.

4.5

The *Pike o' Stickle pentagon,* 3m high, is here seen broadside on from the direction of the bridleway, with Pike o' Stickle dome and south scree to the left above. *NY 2738 0640*

4.5

On an approach from the SSE, the *Pike o' Stickle pentagon* now displays a top face slanting up to a point NW in the direction of Stake Pass. *NY 2738 0640*

A cairnfield may be noticed in the valley bottom in this vicinity, but no evidence has emerged to date the cairns to the period of axe production. *Claris and Quartermaine* also found signs of axe chipping sites towards the foot of the fell in this area [1].

Pike o' Stickle wedge

4.6 Recumbent wedge stone ⇒ *SW to The Band and Oxendale*

NW more large stones are prominent. A long strip of grey scree – the Pike o' Stickle south scree - now stretches down the hillside from the axe working site at Pike o' Stickle. Directly below, and opposite the end corner of the stone wall on the SW side of the track, a few paces from the bridleway, lies a large, recumbent, horizontal stone with a pinkish tinge, and speckled with lichen. Its thinner wedge end is aligned SW again across Mickleden Beck, in the direction of the present footbridge, suggesting the way across the foot of The Band to Oxendale, Red Tarn and Wrynose Pass.

4.7 Triangular profile block ⇒ *WNW to Rossett Gill/SSW to The Band*

About 40 paces to the NW sits another prominent block. When seen broadside on from the SW, the profile of its top ridge seems to imitate the ridge of Langdale Fell above. From an ESE standpoint it displays a clear triangular profile, pointing WNW to the hillside by Rossett Gill.

If these last two stones are viewed from a little further off up the hillside behind, they both reveal pointed profiles aligned across the valley. The last stone now displays a concave back, which slopes up to a wide, rounded tip aligned in a SSW direction across towards the hillside opposite again.

North way up to Troughton Beck chipping sites

Although further prominent rocks on the slope of Langdale Fell invite examination, we will for the moment return to the main track to continue our preliminary reconnaissance. So long as the bridleway continues along the flat valley floor, there are scant signs of stone waymarks. However, further along below Stickle Breast, we can pick up initial markers of a north route past Pike o' Stickle up beside Troughton Beck.

4.8 Upright triangular block ⇒ *NNW up by Troughton Beck*

NW past the foot of the Pile o' Stickle south scree, a large block, with an upright flat triangular face and smooth, flat, slanting sides, sits in front of a low hillock. Along its ridge it points NNW up the hillside in a line leading up across Troughton Beck towards Mart Crag and Stake Pass.

NNW and north up the hillside from here, at least three further northerly pointers may be found. High up this way, to the east of Troughton Beck, were further axe workings, and these markers surely indicated the route to them.

4.6

A *recumbent wedge stone,* below the south scree, points SW across The Band towards Oxendale. *NY 2724 0645*

4.7

Seen broadside on, the top ridge of this stone seems to mimic the profile of the ridge above. End on it points WNW to Rossett Gill, and from above it suggests a way SSW. *NY 2720 0645*

4.8
An *upright triangular block* at the foot of a low hillock, points NNW up the hillside towards Mart Crag and Stake Pass. *NY 2684 0675*

The Rossett Gill Way, and the way south

The bridleway draws alongside Mickleden Beck, and crosses the dry bed of Troughton Beck. Two likely waymark stones appear, spaced about nine paces apart, to the right of the track.

4.9 Upright triangular profile block ⇒ WNW up Rossett Gill

The largest of the two, on the right on a little brow, shows a good rounded triangular profile, and an uneven ridged top, when approached end on from the SE. Its flattish back leans forward and points the way WNW along its ridge up Rossett Gill. This suggests that an ancient route up Rossett Gill proceeded directly WNW from here across Mickleden Beck, cutting off a corner on the modern track - which continues for a while along the NE side of the beck before forking left at the footbridge across Stake Beck. The pass at the top of Rossett Gill gives access to a natural route NW via Angle Tarn, Sprinkling Tarn and Sty Head.

4.9

At the crossing of the dry bed of Troughton Beck, another *triangular profile block* is aligned WNW up to Rossett Gill. *NY 2660 0698*

4.10

At the same crossing, a *recumbent lozenge stone* points due east towards the foot of Gimmer Crag. *NY 2660 0697*

4.10 Recumbent lozenge stone ⇒ *east to Loft Crag*

The left hand stone, a recumbent lozenge, is seen from the far side to point in the opposite direction - due east towards the foot of Gimmer Crag - suggesting a way from the Rossett Gill direction to the Loft Crag, Dungeon Ghyll and Harrison Stickle stone axe working sites.

4.11 Upright lozenge topped block ⇒ *SSE to The Band*

Another substantial stone with a distinct lozenge shaped top can be seen just a little along the beck below, in the far side of the actual bed of the beck. The upper tip of its top points SSE to The Band.

4.11
In the far edge of Mickleden Beck, *a lozenge topped block* points SSE to The Band. *NY 2656 0694*

The Mart Crag Pentagon Group

Further along the bridleway, Mickleden Beck bends nearby under the track again, and a tiny gill comes down the hillside under the track. A cluster of four prominent stones appears amongst other boulders just to the right of the track. All four are large stones, with flat surfaces suggestive of directional alignments. This group of stones may have served as major crossroads waymarks for the routes past the head of the valley.

4.12 Standing pentagonal block ⇒ north to Mart Crag

The first block with upright sides is the largest. Seen from the south below on the track it presents a pentagonal profile, its ridge slanting upwards, due north towards Mart Crag. This gives the impression of a symbolic Mart Crag marker, comparable to the Pike o' Stickle Pentagon. The way beyond in this direction lies directly to Stake Pass, Langstrath and the way north to Borrowdale. *Plint* identified an axe chipping site at Mart Crag [2]; but *Claris and Quartermaine* could not find evidence of a site [3].

4.13 Recumbent lozenge stone ⇒ east to Loft Crag

The next stone northwards along the track is a recumbent one. Its flat lozenge top has its upper rounded tip aligned east up to Loft Crag. This way leads past the foot of the Pike o' Stickle buttresses, and the stone could have marked the way to this important axe working site for travellers down Little Gill or Rossett Gill.

4.14 Recumbent lozenge block ⇒ WNW to Little Gill Head

Next along the path lies a recumbent block with a flattish, elongated lozenge shaped top slanting sideways. Its long point indicates WNW up by Little Gill Head, suggesting a way over the hilltop in the direction of Glaramara, where further chipping sites have been identified.

4.15 Upright, leaf arrowhead topped block ⇒ to the NW side of Pike o' Stickle

Above and behind the last two stones, stands a higher block, with a slanting, flattish leaf arrowhead style top. It slants gently up to a point in an ENE direction beside the NW side of Pike o' Stickle. This suggests a way to give access round that side of Pike o' Stickle to all the axe workings in the Pikes, from the Rossett Gill direction.

Other possible waymark stones may be detected in the vicinity, but not so prominent or distinctly shaped. Further stones which may be waymarks, continue to occur near the bridleway as it approaches the Stake Gill footbridge. They comprise further indicators for routes already identified – one more pointing up Rossett Gill, two north up to Martcrag Moor, and a further one ENE past the nearside of Pike o' Stickle.

Then we arrive at the wooden footbridge over Stake Gill, after which modern directions are marked on a stone slab for the diverging paths - left to Esk Hause, right to Stake Pass. The potential megalithic waymarks that we have encountered have already given strong indications of onward routes in similar directions to those marked near the footbridge – WNW up Rossett Gill towards Angle Tarn and the west; and north up to Stake Pass, Langstrath and Borrowdale.

4.12

This *standing pentagonal block* 1.5m high - one of the group of four stones at the foot of the Mart Crag fellside – shows a ridge and point aligned north up to Mart Crag. *NY 2643 0716*

4.13
A *recumbent lozenge stone* points east past Pike o' Stickle breast; the Mart Crag pentagon stands behind. *NY 2642 0717*

4.14
A *recumbent block* with an *elongated lozenge top,* points up the track in a WNW line, which leads on up the fellside at the head of the valley to Little Gill Head. *NY 2642 0717*

4.15

The *flat leaf arrowhead style top* of this large stone can be seen to be aligned ENE up to the ridge on the near (NW) side of Pike o' Stickle, visible in the distance. *NY 2642 0717*

Table 4a

Guidestones, and directions pointed in Chapter 4

Guide stone no.	Type	Align-ment	Situation	Guide stone rating
⇒	**Pointers to the axe working sites**			
4.3	Upright triangular block	10°	low fell by spring	***
4.5	Standing pentagonal block	10°	fell foot	****
4.10	Recumbent lozenge stone	90°	by gill crossing	**
4.13	Recumbent lozenge stone	90°	fell foot by beck	**
4.15	Upright leaf arrowhead block	60°	fell foot by beck	***
⇒	**Pointers to Wrynose Pass**			
4.3	Upright triangular block	190°	lower fell by spring	***
4.5	Standing pentagonal block	220°	fell foot	****
4.6	Recumbent wedge stone	220°	fell foot	**
4.7	Triangular profile block	220°	fell foot	***
⇒	**Pointers to Rossett Hause**			
4.2	Recumbent lozenge block	270°	by gill	*
4.4	Slanting triangular sided block	290°	low fell by spring	***
4.7	Upright triangular profile block	295°	fell foot	***
4.9	Upright triangular profile block	300°	by beck crossing	***
⇒	**Pointers to Stake Pass**			
4.5	Standing pentagonal block	330°	fell foot	****
4.8	Upright triangular block	340°	at foot of hillock	**
4.12	Standing pentagonal block	360°	fell foot near beck	****
⇒	**Pointer to Little Gill Head**			
4.14	Recumbent lozenge block	290°	fell foot near beck	**
⇒	**Pointer to Blea Tarn**			
4.1	Recumbent pentagon top block	150°	by gill	**
4.11	Upright lozenge topped block	150°	in edge of beck	**
⇒	**Pointer down the valley**			
4.4	Upright triangular sided block	90°	low fell by spring	***

Summary: The Mickleden Way

At the foot of the axe factories

Here in Mickleden we have arrived at the foot of the axe factories. In the valley bottom the Borrowdale tuff occurs, and some chipping sites have been identified. A cairnfield occurs here, at present undated.

Directions indicated (Table 4a)

Up to the axe workings

Two of the most conspicuous megaliths near the valley bottom in Mickleden indicate ways up to the axe working sites on the Pike o' Stickle ridge, from approaches other than up the valley. These include the upright triangular block (4.3) (to Gimmer Crag); and the Pike o' Stickle pentagon (4.5) (to the ridge and gullies), both indicating a way for anyone coming from Wrynose Pass via the foot of The Band. They provide a reminder that, in addition to those coming up Great Langdale, other people came from the south across from Little Langdale and SW from Wrynose Pass to the axe working sites, and they would have little option but to approach the high Pike o' Stickle working sites from the foot of Langdale Fell.

From Mickleden below Stickle Breast, one possible guidestone indicates a northerly trail up Troughton Beck to the axe workings up that way (4.8).

Three further stones towards the head of Mickleden suggest ways from the west via Rossett Hause to the axe working sites. They include two possible markers which suggest the way towards Loft Crag – (4.10 and 4.13), and a probable guidestone (4.15) pointing towards the NW side of Pike o' Stickle.

Arterial routes

From Mickleden, below the Pikes, waymarks can now be picked out for routes fanning out in several directions, as follows:

South and SW via Oxendale and Red Tarn to Wrynose Pass

Four stones, all with 3 star ratings or more, have a clear orientation SW across the valley – suggesting a route across The Band via Oxendale towards Browney Gill, Red Tarn and Wrynose Pass (4.3, 4.5, 4.6, 4.7). This pass would have provided a natural route to Eskdale and the west; and also to Dunnerdale and the SW.

NW route to Rossett Hause, Sty Head and the west

A way up the valley west, across towards Rossett Gill and Esk Hause is also indicated by three probable waymarks (4.4, 4.7, and 4.9), and one more tentative one (4.2).

North route to Stake Pass and Borrowdale

Two strongly rated stones provide indications of the north route from Mickleden up via Stake Pass to Langstrath and Borrowdale. The Pike o' Stickle pentagon (4.5) has a slanting top face suggesting that a route sets out diagonally up the hillside NW towards Mart Crag and Stake Pass. The Mart Crag pentagon (4.12) also suggests a north route.

NW route via Little Gill Head to Glaramara
One stone also suggests a way directly ahead at the top of the valley via Little Gill Head in the Glaramara direction – although is not a very substantial stone and must be regarded as a tentative marker (4.14).

SE to Blea Tarn
Stone 4.1 indicates this direction, although again not a strong marker.

Down the valley
The huge triangular topped stone (4.4) emphatically indicates the way back down the valley.

Locations
Consistency is maintained in the appearance of the stones along the lower slopes of the hillside; and often by gills. Examples have occurred again of stones positioned on a brow to attract attention.

Stone types and groups (Table 4b)
Three substantial *standing blocks* have been identified in this section: the standing triangular block at the foot of Langdale Fell (4.3); the Pike o' Stickle pentagon (4.5); and the Mart Crag pentagon (4.12).

Six stones with good *triangular* shapes have occurred (4.3 (large upright block), 4.4 (large triangular sided block), 4.6 (with a wedge shaped top), 4.7, 4.8, 4.9). Sometimes the triangular shape occurs broadside on; sometimes in the end profile, and sometimes on the top surface.

Six *lozenge* shaped blocks have been identified (4.2, 4.10, 4.11, 4.13, 4.14, 4.15)

Two notable standing stone *pentagonal* blocks have provided outstanding features – the great standing pentagon below Pike o' Stickle (4.5); and another impressive pentagonal specimen below Mart Crag (4.12). A slanting pentagon topped block has also been noticed at Grave Gill (4.1).

One stone has presented a top profile, broadside on, remarkably similar to that of Langdale Fell top above (4.7).

Spaced pairs of large blocks have occurred more than once. A mother and baby *pair* has occurred again (4.1 and 4.2). A cluster of four apparent waymarks has occurred near the head of the valley.

Table 4b

Stone types and features – Chapter 4

Stone no.	Type	Size	Features	Map ref. (NY)
	Standing stones			
4.5	Standing pentagonal block	3.0m H	prominent between gills	2738 0640
4.12	Standing pentagonal block	1.5m H	standing stone; 1 of 4	2643 0716
	Triangular stones			
4.3	Upright triangular block	2.0m H	paired with 4.4	2750 0636
4.4	Upright / slanting triangular sided block	3.0m L	paired with 4.3	2750 0637
4.6	Recumbent wedge topped block	2.2m L	conspicuous	2724 0645
4.7	Upright triangular profile block	1.7m H	hilltop shaped	2720 0645
4.8	Upright triangular faced block	1.1m H		2684 0675
4.9	Upright triangular profile block	1.3m H		2660 0698
	Lozenge / diamond stones			
4.2	Recumbent lozenge topped block	0.7m H	paired with 4.1	2764 0618
4.10	Recumbent lozenge block	2.0m L	paired with 4.9	2660 0697
4.11	Upright lozenge topped block	1.5m H		2656 0694
4.13	Recumbent lozenge block	1.9m L	1 of 4	2642 0717
4.14	Recumbent lozenge block	1.7m L	1 of 4	2642 0717
4.15	Upright / slanting lozenge topped block	1.6m H	1 of 4	2642 0717
	Pentagonal stones			
4.1	Upright / slanting pentagonal topped block	1.5m L	paired with 4.2	2764 0618
4.5	Standing pentagonal block	*see*	*standing stones above*	
4.12	Standing pentagonal block	*see*	*standing stones above*	

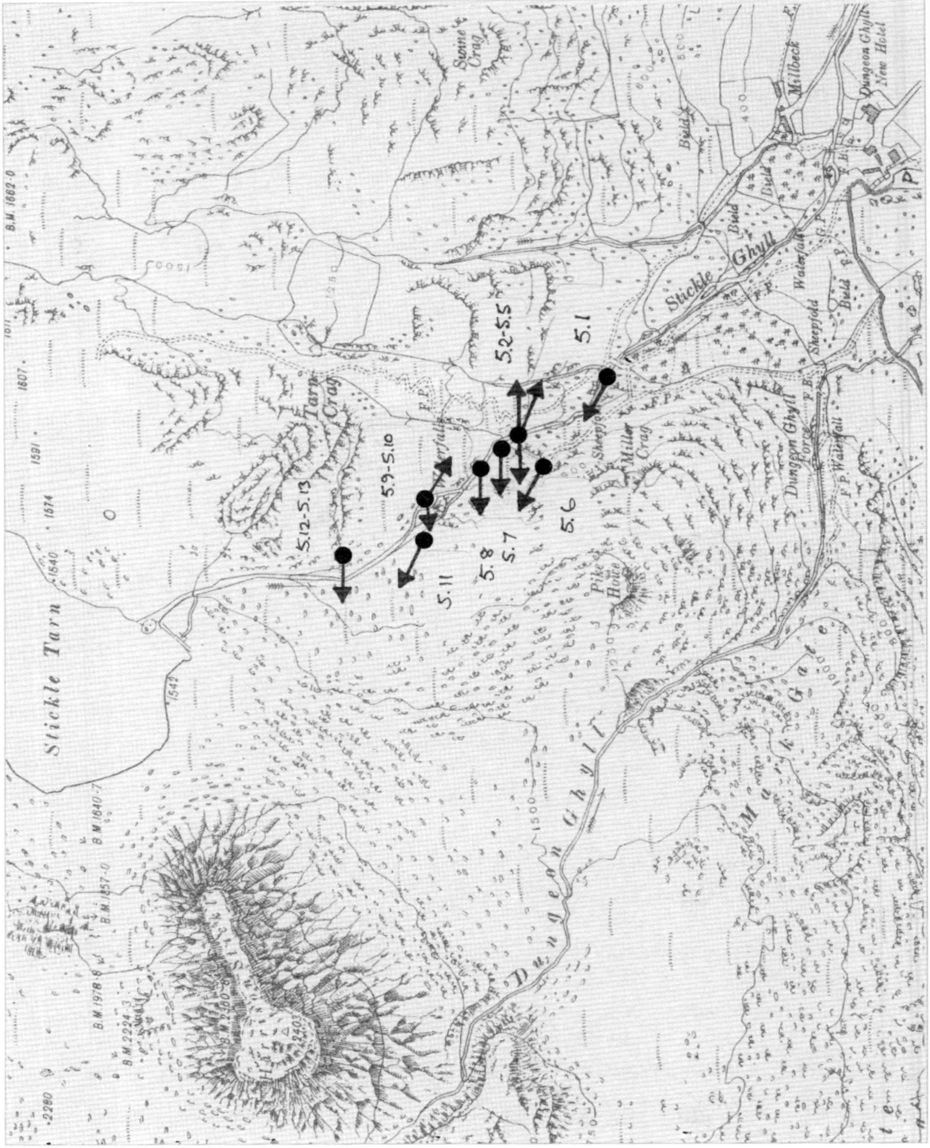

The waterfall way to the axe working sites, showing locations and alignments of stones 5.1 – 5.13 (Chapter 5)

PART 2
THE WATERFALL WAY TO THE AXE WORKING SITES

5 WAYS ACROSS THE STICKLE GHYLL WATERFALLS

Several pointers from the Great Langdale valley up to the axe working sites have been identified in previous chapters. First, at the end of chapter 2, it was noted that one of the longstones at Millbeck suggested a route up across Stickle Ghyll towards Harrison Stickle. This way – a natural one for people coming up the valley from the Windermere direction - will now be explored.

At the last brow on the B road westward before New Dungeon Ghyll Hotel, the main waterfall on Stickle Ghyll comes into view high up the fellside. Stickle Ghyll would have been a significant landmark for the ancient people. Its waterfalls stand out prominently on the hillside above. At the top of the gill, but hidden from the valley below, lies Stickle Tarn. Signs of axe working sites have been found in three locations around the tarn [1]. It seems likely that the shores of the tarn provided the focal point where the axe makers coming from the east and south pitched their summer camps [2]. The grassy moorland around the tarn would provide grazing for their flocks; with the majestic curve of Pavey Ark providing some shelter from the west winds. The axe stone sources were easily accessible nearby.

1st waterfall

A public right of way leads west below the upper longstone at Millbeck (2.13) to Millbeck Farm. At the path T junction past the farm, the path to the right leads up Millbeck towards Stickle Ghyll. In a while the stone wall on the left drops away, and the path from Millbeck merges with the main path up Stickle Ghyll from the Great Langdale car park. Above here, Stickle Ghyll descends the steep hillside in a series of spectacular waterfalls. Six main falls may be distinguished, and possible waymarks around these will now be explored.

5.1 Upright lozenge block ⇒ up NE side of Pike Howe

From the merger of the paths up from Stickle Ghyll and Millbeck, above a gate on the Stickle Ghyll path, the main path upward crosses over a tributary gill. From here, beyond the gill crossing, a likely upstream marker – a substantial lozenge block - may be seen down in the middle of Stickle Ghyll, sitting propped up high on another rock. Seen from the east side, its steeply slanting flat face is rendered more distinctive by streaks of quartz. It points in a significant WNW alignment, which leads off to the left of the stream, up the NE side of Pike Howe, towards Harrison Stickle.

This area of Stickle Ghyll provides easy access at either side for a crossing point from SE to NW. Large stepping stones now provide a way across the stream here for twenty-first century visitors. Across the stepping stones, a path carries on up the west side of the gill.

5.1

This *lozenge block,* propped up on another rock in Stickle Ghyll, points WNW up the side of Pike Howe towards Harrison Stickle. *NY 2914 0687*

A closer view of this lozenge block reveals its thick diagonal streaks.

Off this path to the right round the bottom of a fence, the first main waterfall presents a beautiful sight ahead.

2nd waterfall

On up past the first falls, a second substantial waterfall over reddish brown rock looms up ahead.

5.2 Triangular standing stone ⇒ east down the side of the valley

In profile on the very edge of the top of the waterfall a striking triangular stone stands up conspicuously, its top curving up to a point like a jester's hat. By clambering up on the left side of the falls, a ledge may be reached to give access for a closer view. Now from a westerly viewpoint it displays a slim lozenge style profile, with a ridge slanting up in an easterly direction, marking the way across the top of the waterfall and along the side of the valley (though not via Millbeck, but higher up the fellside past the foot of Scout Crag).

It would be remarkable if this standing stone had ended up in this position, perched upright on the top edge of the waterfall, by natural forces. It has all the appearance of a stone positioned by human hand.

A crossing may conveniently be made here across the top of the waterfall.

3rd waterfall

If we climb up the bank on the east side, and overlook the stream, a little way up, towards the next pretty, smaller waterfall above, a pair of large stones, only about a metre apart stand out conspicuously below on the bank on the far side of the stream.

5.3 Upright triangular block ⇒ west to Harrison Path/South to Side Pike

When viewed broadside on from the east side, the first one offers a steeply slanting triangular face and chiselled top pointing in a westerly direction.

5.4 Slanting longstone ⇒ west to Harrison path

The other stone is more impressive - a substantial, elongated lozenge style longstone, lying at a slant up the bank of the beck, with a concave top and a distinct upper point. It is aligned in a direction just slightly north of west up the hillside, pointing a route leading straight in the direction of the Harrison path to the axe working sites.

When seen from our viewpoint on the high bank overlooking the stream on the east side, the alignment of this prominent stone leads the eye up the hillside beside a little gill to the ridge above. Here are a pair of megaliths clearly marking the way across Stickle Ghyll below the third falls, and west up to the ridge above – the way to the axe working sites. They appear to have been positioned here so as to be conspicuous on an approach up this easterly bank of the stream.

5.2

A triangular standing stone - the 'jester's hat' – perches on the top edge of the second Stickle Ghyll waterfall. A rock climbing party below prepare to ascend the waterfall. *NY 2906 0700*

This view beside the 'jester's hat' on top of the waterfall, shows its easterly alignment across the falls.

5.3 and **5.4**
Viewed from up above on the east bank of the stream, this *upright triangular block* and *slanting longstone*, by the edge of Stickle Ghyll, point the way west up to the Pike Howe ridge above. *NY 2904 0702*

5.3
The *upright triangular block* – a closer view

5.4
The *slanting longstone* seen from the south side

5.5

This *lozenge topped block* below the third waterfall, is propped up at the front on another block, and points the way ESE down the valley. *NY 2904 0702*

5.6

A *diamond sided block* points NW in the direction of Harrison Stickle. *NY 2900 0695*

5.5 Recumbent lozenge topped block ⇒ ESE down the valley to Millbeck longstones

On a low rock outcrop on the nearside of the stream, not far upstream, and a little below the next falls, an altogether smaller upright block could go unnoticed, except that it displays a flat, well-shaped, lozenge top gently rising to a point ESE down the valley in the direction of the Millbeck longstones. The stone is propped up at the front on another stone.

5.6 Upright diamond sided block ⇒ WNW to Harrison Stickle/Pike Howe ridge

A little way up the hillside west from the waterfall here, a block with a smooth flat face and the sharp profile of a diamond on its side stands out conspicuously. On closer inspection it is seen to lie in front of a rock outcrop, and to have an elongated face more in the shape of a rectangle. It points 300° WNW from end point to end point - towards Harrison Stickle; or 285° north of west up to the ridge along its sharp straight ridge. Here is a strong indicator of a way up from the waterfalls WNW to the ridge above Pike Howe.

From the top of the second falls to the top of the third, at least five potential waymarks have been identified. Two of the stones have indicated an east or ESE direction; and two emphatic pointers, plus a third up the hillside nearby, indicate the WNW way up to the ridge. A likely crossing point from Millbeck across Stickle Ghyll is suggested in this vicinity, up to the Pike Howe ridge. This way will be picked up in the next section.

Meanwhile, we will first explore further upstream. At each of the three main waterfalls above here, and beyond up Stickle Ghyll, further likely waymarks can be identified. Whilst other directions, for example NE past Tarn Crag, are marked, it is striking how often westerly pointers occur.

4th waterfall

5.7 Upright lozenge topped block ⇒ west to outcrop on Pike Howe ridge

If the third waterfall is skirted on the left hand side, at the outcrop above a fourth waterfall close above, an upright block nearly a metre and a half high displays a slanting lozenge top with an upper point due west towards an outcrop visible on the ridge above.

5th waterfall

5.8 Standing pentagon block ⇒ west up to Pike Howe ridge

If the way is pursued up the west side of Stickle Ghyll off the path, the top of a fifth significant waterfall is reached. Half way between this waterfall and the final great spidery falls above, a block with a pentagonal profile and a scooped back stands upright in the west edge of Stickle Ghyll. It points due west again over its pointed top, up a tributary gill, to the ridge above.

5.7

The *lozenge topped block* above the fourth waterfall is here viewed from above. It points due west towards an outcrop on the Pike Howe ridge above. *NY 2900 0703*

5.8

The standing pentagonal block in the foreground, with a scooped back, also points due west up a gill to the Pike Howe ridge above. The sixth waterfall cascades down in the background. *NY 2899 0705*

5.9

This *slanting, lozenge topped block,* resembling a leaf arrowhead, sits in the top of the sixth and highest waterfall. It points the way ESE down Great Langdale. *NY 2896 0713*

5.9 and **5.10**

The two stones in the foreground are the *lozenge topped block* (5.9) on the right, and an *upright triangular block* (5.10) on the left. The latter points just south of west up to the Pike Howe ridge. *NY 2896 0713*

6th waterfall

5.9 Slanting lozenge topped block ⇒ *ESE down the valley*

If we now cross to the east side of the stream above the top of the spider falls, a fine specimen may be seen in the central area of the main stream above the top of the falls: a block with a flat, well shaped lozenge top, resembling a leaf arrowhead. This top surface slants sideways and backwards, with its upper tip pointing ESE down Great Langdale towards Lake Windermere, which can now be seen in the distance. Here is a dramatically placed waymark indicating the long distance direction of travel down the valley.

5.10 Upright triangular block ⇒ *WSW up to Pike Howe ridge*

Nearby in the stream, on the NE side of this stone, a triangular block stands upright, giving a line just south of west towards the Pike Howe ridge when viewed from the east side.

5.11 Twin pointed upright lozenge block ⇒ *WNW up to Pike Howe ridge*

A large stone stands out, perched on cobbles, on the west side of Stickle Ghyll above the waterfall. When approached from the SE, it presents a nearly vertical face, slightly stepped, and a twin pointed top profile pointing WNW up to a dip in the ridge above. The triangular profile of another stone stands out blackly on the ridge in the distance, providing a foresight in this direction. The way to it up the hillside is not difficult: here lay another route to the ridge above. The stone on the ridge will be visited in the next section.

5.11

This large *twin pointed lozenge block* is perched on a bed of cobbles on the west side of Stickle Ghyll. Its twin points can be seen to be aligned WNW to the dip in the Pike Howe ridge above. *NY 2885 0713*

Stickle Tarn path

5.12 Recumbent lozenge block ⇒ West to Harrison path and Pike o' Stickle

The path towards Stickle Tarn on the east side of Stickle Ghyll will now be taken beyond the spider falls, as far as the bend to the right below the corner of Tarn Crag. A large recumbent thick slab with a flattish, crudely rounded lozenge shape top slants up due west, to the dip in the ridge and the visible end of Harrison Stickle. Significantly, this direction leads directly to the Harrison path and the pass between Thorn Crag and Harrison Stickle, giving access to Pike o' Stickle.

5.13 Triangular ended block ⇒ WNW to ridge and Stickle Tarn

Three steps above, a long recumbent stone with a triangular profile leaning on another, points an easy route north of west up to the ridge above.

If the way indicated by this stone is followed, it leads up a steep, steady, grassy and brackeny hillside with a protruding natural rock outcrop for a foresight ahead. Possible waymarks may be identified en route. Up on the top, further likely waymarks on the path to Stickle Tarn are reached, and an easy way to the SW edge of the tarn.

5.12

A *large recumbent slab*, crudely rounded lozenge in shape, at the bend below the corner of Tarn Crag, slants up to a point aligned due west. *NY 2887 0721*

5.13

The upper stone, *triangular in profile*, is a recumbent longstone, aligned in a WNW direction, which gives an easy route up to the ridge. *NY 2887 0721*

Table 5a
Guidestones, and directions pointed in Chapter 5

Guide stone no.	Type	Align-ment	Situation	Guide stone rating
⇒	**Pointers to Harrison Stickle west site**			
5.1	Upright lozenge block	300°	in mid stream	****
5.3	Upright triangular block	270°	on west bank of stream	***
5.4	Slanting longstone	270°	on west bank of stream	***
5.6	Upright/slanting diamond sided block	300°	fellside near outcrop	**
⇒	**Pointers to Harrison Stickle east site**			
5.7	Upright lozenge topped block	270°	at outcrop above 4th falls	**
5.8	Standing pentagonal block	270°	in west edge of stream	***
5.10	Upright triangular block	260°	on top of 6th falls	***
5.11	upright twin pointed lozenge block	295°	on west side of stream	***
5.12	Recumbent lozenge block	270°	at corner/foot of Tarn Crag	**
⇒	**Pointers to Stickle Tarn sites**			
5.13	Triangular profile block	285°	at corner/foot of Tarn Crag	**
⇒	**Pointers down the valley**			
5.2	Triangular standing stone	90°	on top of 2nd falls	****
5.5	Slanting lozenge topped block	110°	below 3rd falls	**
5.9	Slanting lozenge topped block	120°	on top of 6th falls	***

Summary: Ways across the Stickle Ghyll Waterfalls

Locations
The multiple waterfalls on Stickle Ghyll provide one of the most dramatic natural water features in the Lake District. The falls were apparently used by the ancient people to draw attention to likely guidestones. In two cases, waymark stones have been positioned at the very tops of the waterfalls (5.2 and 5.9). Altogether no less than five stones have been found positioned in the actual bed of the stream, and most of the others on the nearby banks. One large pair on the west bank are positioned so as to be conspicuous when seen on an approach from down the valley up to the bank of the stream on the east side (5.3 and 5.4).

In three instances, stones point the way up beside a tributary gill west or WNW up to the ridge behind Pike Howe (5.3, 5.4 and 5.8). Further stones or rock outcrops on the brow of the ridge above, appear to have provided foresights to allow travellers up the slope to maintain a steady course.

The likely guidestones suggest that the Neolithic axe makers came up the valley to Millbeck, then headed for the Stickle Ghyll waterfalls and on up WNW to the ridge behind Pike Howe. The onward ways from the ridge will be explored in the next two sections.

Directions indicated (Table 5a)
The Stickle Ghyll waterfalls have provided the setting for several distinctive likely waymarks. It is remarkable how many of these indicate ways up via the Pike Howe ridge in the direction of the axe working sites. Three main ways towards the axe working sites may be distinguished.

Up to Harrison Stickle (West site) via lower end of ridge
The first high triangular block points WNW up towards the Pike Howe ridge (5.1). From the area below the third waterfall, the upright triangular block and large longstone on the west bank of the stream point a WNW way by a gill up the hillside to the ridge, in a line which leads on to the Harrison path to the axe working sites (5.3 and 5.4). All three of these stones have a strong guidestone rating. The diamond sided block (a more tentative waymark a little way up the hillside here) suggests a similar direction (5.6).

Up to Harrison Stickle (East site) via middle of ridge
Further upstream, stones indicate a westerly way up to the ridge. The three strongest likely waymarks include the standing pentagon between the fifth and sixth waterfalls pointing up another gill up the hillside (5.8); the standing triangle in the top of the sixth falls (5.10) and the twin pointed lozenge stone past the sixth falls (5.11). Other possible guidestones are a possible lozenge topped block near the top of the fourth waterfall, which points in the direction of an outcrop on the ridge above (5.7); and the recumbent lozenge further up the Stickle Tarn path (5.12).

Up to Stickle Tarn via upper end of ridge
From up the Stickle Tarn path, at the corner below Tarn Crag, a tentative guidestone in the form of a recumbent stone with a triangular profile marks the way WNW from here in the Stickle Tarn direction (5.13).

Down the valley
Three stones, all associated with waterfalls, have indicated the way back east or ESE down the valley. Two of them rate strongly as probable guidestones: the jester's hat on top of the second falls (5.2); and the slanting leaf arrowhead/kite shaped stone at the top of the sixth falls (5.9). A third possible waymark is the modest but well shaped lozenge topped stone below the third falls (5.5).

Stone types and groups (Table 5b)
Five blocks with striking *triangular* profiles have been found: the first high, streaked block in the midst of the stream (5.1); the standing jester's hat on the top of the second waterfall (5.2); the large stone paired with a longstone below the third waterfall (5.3); the standing block on top of the sixth waterfall (5.10); and the recumbent stone with a triangular profile at the corner below Tarn Crag (5.13).

The *lozenge* shape usually occurs on the tops of the stones in this section. It is represented by a modest block below the third waterfall (5.5); a larger lozenge topped block near the fourth waterfall (5.7); a sharply defined kite shaped pointer in the top of the sixth waterfall (5.9); a conspicuous lozenge stone with a *double pointed* profile (5.11); and a crudely shaped, wide recumbent version further up the Stickle Tarn path (5.12).

One *pentagonal* example has occurred: a standing stone with a pentagonal profile, standing in the stream between the fifth and sixth waterfalls (5.8).

One very large *longstone* has been identified (5.6)
Stones have occurred in pairs below the third waterfall (5.3 and 5.4), and on top of the sixth falls (5.9 and 5.10), and again further up the Stickle Tarn path (5.12 and 5.13).

Table 5b

Stone types and features – Chapter 5

Stone no.	Type	Size	Features	Map ref. (NY)
▯	**Standing stones**			
5.2	Standing triangular block	1.9m H	prominent standing stone	2906 0700
5.8	Standing pentagonal block	1.5m H	standing stone	2899 0705
5.11	Upright double pointed block	1.8m H	quasi standing stone	2885 0713
△	**Triangular stones**			
5.1	Upright lozenge block	1.9m H	streaked propped up	2914 0687
5.2	Standing triangular block	*see*	*standing stones above*	
5.3	Upright triangular block	1.8m H	paired with 5.4	2904 0702
5.10	Upright triangular block	1.6m H	paired with 5.9	2896 0713
5.13	triangular profile block	2.6m L	paired with 5.12; propped up	2887 0721
◇	**Lozenge/diamond stones**			
5.4	Slanting longstone	2.8m L	paired with 5.3	2904 0702
5.5	Slanting lozenge topped block	0.8m H	propped up	2904 0702
5.6	Upright/slanting diamond sided block	2.2m L		2900 0695
5.7	Upright lozenge topped block	1.4m H		2900 0703
5.9	Slanting lozenge topped block	1.8m L	paired with 5.10	2896 0713
5.12	Recumbent lozenge block	2.1m L	paired with 5.13	2887 0721
⬠	**Pentagonal stones**			
5.8	Standing pentagonal block	*see*	*standing stones above*	

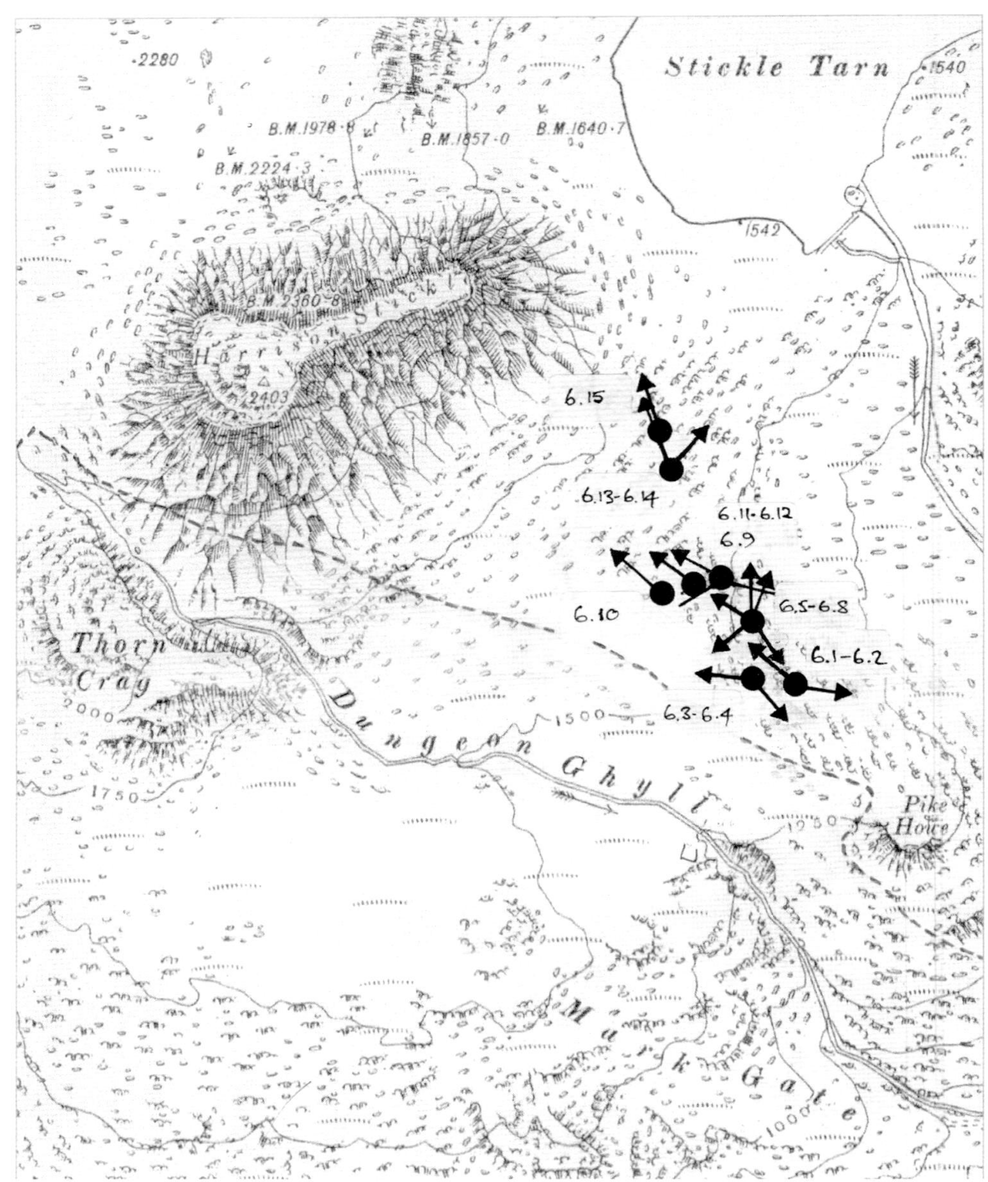

Ways to Stickle Tarn and the Harrison Stickle axe working sites, showing locations and alignments of stones 6.1 – 6.15 (chapter 6)

6 WAYS TO STICKLE TARN AND THE HARRISON STICKLE AXE WORKING SITES

The first way up from Stickle Ghyll waterfalls

In this chapter the line WNW is followed up the fellside, as prompted by several stones near the third waterfall (5.3, 5.4 and 5.6). Possible guidestones (not included in this text) may be noticed on the way up the fellside. The going is not difficult, but steep in places, up the grassy course of a tiny gill. The main likely waymarks are to be found at the next natural feature – the brow of the ridge above. After climbing up over a steep brow, a standing stone (6.1 below) becomes visible in the distance as a foresight, just below the top ridge, its bright face gleaming in the sun against the blackness of the outcrop behind.

The first outcrop: Arrowhead standing stone group

6.1 Leaf arrowhead standing stone slab ⇒ to SW edge of Stickle Tarn

A substantial, tall stone with a kite shaped/slim leaf arrowhead upright flat face, it points NW to the east end of Harrison Stickle – the way to the SW edge of Stickle Tarn. It may be suggested that this is merely a natural outcrop. However, it appears to be free standing, cracked away from the outcrop adjacent to it. If it is a natural occurrence, then its alignment is a curious coincidence.

6.2 Pointed standing stump ⇒ down the valley/west up Thorn Crag path

Nearby SE, a little below the brow of the hill a four sided stone stump stands at a slant. From a NW viewpoint it presents an upright, fairly flat face leaning sideways northwards; and indicates the way ESE down Great Langdale, visible below.

When seen from the east from an approach up the hillside below, it indicates due west over its crudely triangular upper surface and rounded tip - the way to the foot of Thorn Crag, giving access to the Thorn Crag path up to the stone working sites at Loft Crag and Pike o' Stickle.

6.3 Recumbent/slanting longstone ⇒ WNW up Harrison path

On the brow above sit a close pair of large stones, isolated in the turf. Seen from the east below, the larger one – a substantial stone nearly 4m long - is aligned lengthwise just north of west - the way up in the direction of the Harrison path beside Dungeon Ghyll, towards the major axe making sites. Its end point is turned slightly towards Harrison Stickle. This way up the Harrison path will be explored in chapter 7.

6.4 Slanting lozenge slab ⇒ SE down Pike Howe path

The other stone, propped up against the first, reveals its shape and alignment from a viewpoint round to the north. It points SE - the way down the present Pike Howe path to the Great Langdale car parks. It displays a well-defined lozenge shape, with a slanting back and cut away lower corner. A little baby diamond stone next to it is, perhaps significantly, aligned in the same direction.

6.1
A substantial *leaf arrowhead stone slab* stands over 3m high at the first outcrop, its point aligned NW to the east end of Harrison Stickle. *NY 2874 0700*

6.2
A *pointed standing stone stump,* a little below the brow of the ridge, indicates the way ESE down Great Langdale, visible below. *NY 2875 0699*

6.3

A large *recumbent longstone* is aligned just north of west in the direction of the Harrison path. The peak of Harrison Stickle rises to the upper right. *NY 2871 0702*

6.4

Paired with the longstone, a *slanting lozenge slab* points the way SE down the present Pike Howe path. *NY 2871 0702*

It is noticeable that these last four stones occur below the brow of the Pike Howe ridge on the NE side – not on the top of the ridge. This implies that they were guidestones on an approach route from the Stickle Ghyll waterfalls, and not from the present path leading up the Pike Howe ridge from Great Langdale car parks - none of them are visible from this path.

The Stickle Tarn path

Nowadays a clear path to Stickle Tarn is worn down just on the top of the ridge behind Pike Howe. However, if the line indicated by the tall standing stone (6.1) is pursued, another, fainter parallel path leading along a natural way northward, a little below the top of the ridge, can be picked up, passing a succession of three further prominent rock outcrops.

Below each of the large outcrops, more likely waymark stones can be found. These include indicators to both the SE and SW edges of Stickle Tarn; and NW up to Harrison Stickle, to the right hand side of its main peak.

The second outcrop

6.5 Upright/slanting pentagon block ⇒ north to Stickle Tarn/ NW to Harrison Stickle

A little way along the faint path the second outcrop rises above, with two spaced old rowan trees below it. A few steps below the first tree, past a spring, a block approached end on presents a slanting pentagonal back pointing due north: a second conspicuous pointer towards the SW corner of Stickle Tarn. However, when seen from the SE side, it displays a strong rounded triangular profile, with a vertical flat face and a point aligned NW up an easy way to Harrison Stickle.

On each side sit smaller possible, but rather doubtful, waymarks. One close by on the SE side, with a flattish slanting lozenge back, points the opposite way south. This way lies in the Blea Tarn direction, via Dungeon Ghyll lower ravine. Another more crudely shaped lozenge stone lies recumbent, close by on the other NW side. It may have been broken off the larger stone; its stepped top is aligned SW/NE. The SW way lies across Dungeon Ghyll to the Mark Gate path.

6.6 Small slanting longstone ⇒ NNE to Stickle Tarn

Towards the upper Rowan tree and the outcrop above, a small ridged longstone is conspicuously propped up so as to protrude at a slant on a rock outcrop. It points NNE in the direction of the east side of Stickle Tarn.

6.7 Recumbent triangular stone ⇒ SE down Pike Howe

A larger, strikingly shaped recumbent triangular stone sits only a little above. Over 2m long, its flattish, more or less horizontal top leads to a sharp point. The stone is aligned SE down the Pike Howe ridge, but the point is turned a little ESE.

6.5

This upright block near the second outcrop, approached end on, presents a *slanting pentagonal profile* pointing due north in the direction of the SW corner of Stickle Tarn. *NY 2863 0707*

The same block, seen broadside on from the SE, now points NW to Harrison Stickle.

6.6
This small *ridged longstone* is propped up to protrude at a slant towards the east side of Stickle Tarn. *NY 2868 0709*

6.7
A sharp pointed triangular stone points down Pike Howe ridge towards the valley. *2867 0708*

6.8 Standing/leaning slab ⇒ *SW to Dungeon Ghyll crossing*

Just above the last, a standing slab leans back from vertical. The alignment, broadside on over its rounded top, lies SW over the moor above in the direction of the Harrison path and/or the Thorn Crag path.

Other possible waymarks may be found nearby above. A large long pointed recumbent stone appears to point NNE to the lip of Stickle Tarn again. On top of this stone sits a crudely lozenge shaped stone with a point aligned SW again like the standing slab.

The third outcrop – and pointers to Harrison Stickle (East site)

6.9 Standing stone slab ⇒ *NW to Harrison Stickle*

The third outcrop above the path has a steep face, and the ground falls away steeply below. Close by its NE foot, a slab of pinkish stone with a spearhead or elongated pentagon profile stands upright. End on it shows a clear top point in a NW alignment towards the right hand side of the peak of Harrison Stickle. This line lies directly to the Harrison Stickle east axe working site.

6.10 Upright lozenge topped block ⇒ *NW to Harrison Stickle*

Up on top of the ridge behind this outcrop, a very conspicuous large block, sits isolated from other stones in the upland grass. A metre and a half high, with a lozenge plan, it has a front end converging to a strong point in the direction of the right hand side of the peak of Harrison Stickle, and the Harrison Stickle East working site again.

The second way up from Stickle Ghyll waterfalls

Down the steep slope ENE below the standing slab, across the path below the ridge, a dip down to the right provides the access up for another main route from Stickle Ghyll – as previously indicated particularly by the twin pointed block above the top waterfall (5.11).

6.11 Triangular profile block ⇒ *ESE down to top waterfall*

Not far downhill sits a large long ridged block below another outcrop. This stone is the one that, with its triangular profile, provided a distant foresight when seen from the twin pointed block below. Seen from that side, it points WSW up its top point over the ridge towards the Harrison path. However, when viewed from behind above to the west, it also shows a triangular profile; and its long ridge shows a prominent ESE alignment down to the top waterfall, visible in the valley below.

6.12 Piggy-back slanting lozenge stone ⇒ *NW to Harrison Stickle east site*

Nearby below another quaint feature appears. A slanting lozenge stone sits piggy-back style on the shoulder of the outcrop below the long rock. Significantly, it points NW, marking the direction of the Harrison Stickle east working site again.

Other tentative waymark stones here include possible north and south markers.

6.8
The rounded top of this *standing/ leaning slab* points SW towards the Harrison path. *NY 2867 0708*

6.9
Another *standing slab* points NW towards the Harrison Stickle east working site. *NY 2860 0716*

6.10
A large block with *a lozenge shaped plan,* is seen here from in front of its pointed end. It points NW towards the Harrison Stickle east working site again. Lingmoor Fell rises in the background across Great Langdale. *NY 2866 0709*

6.11

A long *ridged block with a triangular profile* points ESE down from the ridge to the sixth waterfall on Stickle Ghyll below. *NY 2868 0714*

6.12

A *lozenge stone* sits *piggy-back style* on the top of a larger outcrop. It points the way NW towards the Harrison Stickle east working site. *NY 2867 0717*

6.13

A *slanting triangular pointer block* indicates the way NNW up to the ridge overlooking the west end of Stickle Tarn. *NY 2861 0729*

6.14

On the surface of this *recumbent diamond stone,* several ring markings may be seen. The stone itself points NE in the direction of the east end of Stickle Tarn. *NY 2862 0727*

Pointers to the Stickle Tarn axe working sites

6.13 Upright/slanting triangular block ⇒ NNW to Stickle Tarn west end

Past the fourth outcrop, an upright/slanting, rounded triangular style pointer has now become prominent ahead, on a dip in the next ridge. It sits just past the point where the more distinct modern path from the Pike Howe ridge merges in from the left, and then forks again right. It points the way up to the ridge overlooking the west end of Stickle Tarn.

6.14 Recumbent diamond ring marked stone ⇒ NE to Stickle Tarn east end

Nearby above the main path as it forks right, a recumbent, diamond shaped stone lies uphill below the top of a hillock. It points NE in a line which leads to the lip at the other (east) end of Stickle Tarn. The stone would not be especially remarkable, but for the markings on its face. The flattish top of this reddish stone displays at least five ring markings, with central nodules. They vary from 11cm to 3cm in diameter. Whether natural or made by human hand, they make the stone distinctive.

6.15 Recumbent pentagonal stone ⇒ NNW to Stickle Tarn west end

If the way left towards Pavey Ark marked by the elongated triangle is taken off the main path to Stickle Tarn, another likely waymark appears, close to an outcrop on the right. A large, wide, crudely pentagonal shaped stone lies recumbent up a slope. Extensive criss-cross lines mark the surface of the stone. It points up the ridge ahead. Just above here we arrive at a dip in the ridge where the west end of Stickle Tarn comes into view. A grassy slope leads down to the tarn.

Traces of three small chipping sites have been found in the vicinity of Stickle Tarn [1]. One site lay near the SW corner of the tarn, and another lay at its NW edge. Both of these sites lie directly ahead from the viewpoint we have reached on the ridge above, as a result of following the megalithic pointers. The third site lay at the SE edge of the tarn, in the direction indicated by the ring marked stone (6.14).

6.15
A wide *pentagonal stone* with extensive criss-cross markings, points NNW up over the ridge nearby. At the ridge the west end of Stickle Tarn comes into view. *NY 2859 0733*

Table 6a
Guidestones, and directions pointed in Chapter 6

Guide stone no.	Type	Align- ment	Situation	Guide stone rating
⇒	**Pointers to Stickle Tarn**	**sites**		
6.1	Standing leaf arrowhead slab	310°	in front of outcrop	***
6.5	Upright pentagon block	360°	by path below outcrop	***
6.6	Small slanting longstone	20°	near outcrop	**
6.13	Slanting triangular block	335°	by path in dip on ridge	***
6.14	Recumbent/slanting diamond stone	40°	by path below brow of hillock	***
6.15	Recumbent/slanting pentagonal stone	335°	by outcrop near brow of ridge	*
⇒	**Pointers to Harrison Stickle east site**			
6.5	Upright pentagon block	305°	by path below outcrop	***
6.9	Standing elongated pentagon slab	305°	close up against outcrop face	***
6.10	Upright lozenge topped block	310°	on open moorland	***
6.12	Slanting lozenge stone	300°	on shoulder of outcrop	****
⇒	**Pointers to Harrison Stickle west site**			
6.2	Standing four sided stump	270°	below brow of hill	***
6.3	Recumbent slanting longstone	275°	on edge of ridge	**
6.8	Standing/leaning slab	230°	near outcrop	**
6.11	Triangular profile long block	240°	by outcrop	***
⇒	**Pointers to Windermere**			
6.2	Standing pointed four sided stump	100°	below brow of hill	***
6.11	Triangular profile long block	105°	by outcrop	***
⇒	**Pointers to Coniston**			
6.4	Slanting lozenge slab	145°	on edge of ridge	****

Summary: Ways to Stickle Tarn and Harrison Stickle axe making sites

Locations

This chapter has demonstrated the use of the brow of the hill, with strategically placed waymarks at natural outcrops as foresights to guide travellers. Likely guidestones have been positioned near several natural outcrops, sometimes in clusters. A particular feature has been the positioning of stones below the crags; but sometimes, apparently important waymarks have been located in the moorland grass above. In general, they come into view on an approach up the fellside from Stickle Ghyll.

Directions indicated (Table 6a)

To axe working sites

The megaliths described in this chapter carry considerable significance in pointing onward ways towards three known axe working site areas:

- Stickle Tarn
- Harrison Stickle (east site)
- Harrison Stickle (west site)

They have picked up two routes indicated by stones around the Stickle Ghyll waterfalls below.

To Stickle Tarn

The path along towards the western side of Stickle Tarn, below several rock outcrops, is repeatedly indicated by several substantial and conspicuous blocks (standing stone 6.1, slanting pentagon 6.5, slanting triangular block 6.13, recumbent pentagon 6.15). The first three of these achieve good star ratings. The way to the eastern edge of the tarn is also pointed by two probable guidestones (6.6 and 6.14). These pointers could have considerable significance. After a trek up the fellside the axe makers would not necessarily have proceeded direct to the axe working sites – particularly if they were bringing animal flocks with them. In any new season, it would have been sensible to set up camp at Stickle Tarn, and either exploit the Harrison Stickle east site, or follow the line of successive suitable rock sources winding westwards from this one until a working site deemed suitable for further exploitation had been reached. The strong pointers in the Stickle Tarn direction suggest that the sheltered shores of the tarn may have provided a focal point for this.

Whilst working sites have been found by the tarn, the natural raw material for making axes was probably brought there from the main axe stone sources nearby.

To Harrison Stickle east site

Several stones point up in the direction of the Harrison Stickle east axe working site area (6.5, 6.9, 6.10, 6.12 – the piggy back stone). All of these are rated at 3 stars or above.

To Harrison Stickle west site
The way up the Harrison Path to the Harrison Stickle west site, and the onward path by Dungeon Ghyll to the Pike o' Stickle working sites is also indicated by three likely waymarks: standing stump (6.2), standing/leaning slab (6.8) and possibly the triangular profile longstone (6.11). The large longstone (6.3) is a more tentative pointer.

Here, then, we have a number of megaliths strongly suggestive of waymarks pointing direct to known axe working sites, at Stickle Tarn and Harrison Stickle.

Down the valley via Stickle Ghyll falls to Windermere
Two ways back down to the Stickle Ghyll waterfalls are marked by 3 star stones, matching the ways pointed up from below. The standing stump (6.2) points the first way back via the third waterfall. The long block with a triangular profile (6.11) points the second way directly down to the top of the sixth waterfall.

SE and South to Coniston
Two good specimens indicate the way SE down Pike Howe (6.4 and 6.7), in the Blea Tarn and Coniston direction.

Stone types and groups (Table 6b)
A large leaf arrowhead *standing stone* has been encountered (6.1). Nearby a much smaller standing stump stands below the brow of the ridge (6.2). A standing/leaning slab has occurred close to an outcrop (6.8); and a somewhat inconspicuous pink standing stone stands close up against a crag face (6.9).

A block showing a pentagonal end profile, presents an upright *triangular* face broadside on (6.5). A sharp pointed large recumbent triangular stone has been encountered (6.7). A long block with a triangular profile has occurred (6.11). A prominent block with a slanting triangular profile has also been noted (6.13).

The *lozenge* shape is immediately displayed in the leaf arrowhead style standing stone (6.1). A slanting lozenge slab, with a baby close by has been seen (6.4). A large upright block (6.10) has a lozenge shaped plan; a piggy-back stone repeats the shape (6.12), as does the recumbent, ring marked diamond by the bend in the Stickle Tarn path (6.14).

A *pentagonally* shaped *longstone* occurs (6.3). An upright/slanting specimen is to be found (6.5). A standing stone has been seen with an elongated pentagonal profile (6.9). A large, crudely pentagonal recumbent stone (6.15) is distinguished by criss-cross markings on its surface.

Stones 6.3 and 6.4 provide an example of a close *pair* of stones. Stone 6.4 itself has an additional tiny baby one close by, aligned in the same direction. Stones 6.6, 6.7 and 6.8 form a fairly close group. Some particular paired curiosities have been encountered in this chapter. A ridged triangular block has a paired *piggy-back* stone not far away (6.11, 6.12). A low *ring marked* slab has a paired triangular companion nearby (6.14, 6.13).

Table 6b

Stone types and features – Chapter 6

Stone no.	Type	Size	Features	Map ref. (NY)
▯	**Standing Stones**			
6.1	Standing leaf arrowhead slab	3.2m H	large and prominent; leaf arrowhead style	2874 0700
6.2	Standing four sided stump	1.5m H	near 6.1	2875 0690
6.8	Standing/leaning slab	c1m H	grouped with 2 others	2867 0708
6.9	Standing elongated pentagonal slab	1.3m H	close to crag face	2863 0713
△	**Triangular Stones**			
6.5	Upright/slanting pentagonal block	1.4m H	triangular broadside on	2870 0707
6.7	Recumbent triangular stone	2.2m L	sharp turned point; grouped with 2 others	2867 0708
6.11	Upright triangular profile long block	3.0m L	paired with 6.10	2868 0714
6.13	Triangular profile block	1.5m H	prominent	2861 0729
◇	**Lozenge Stones**			
6.1	Standing leaf arrowhead slab	*see*	*standing stones above*	
6.2	Standing four sided stump	*see*	*standing stones above*	
6.4	Slanting lozenge slab	1.9m L	paired with 6.3; propped up	2871 0702
6.10	Upright lozenge topped block	1.5m H	prominent	2860 0711
6.12	Slanting lozenge stone	0.9m H	piggy-back; paired with 6.11	2867 0717
6.14	Recumbent/slanting diamond stone	1.4m L	ring marked	2862 0727
⬠	**Pentagonal stones**			
6.5	Upright/slanting pentagonal block	*see*	*triangular stones above*	2870 0707
6.9	Standing elongated pentagonal slab	*see*	*standing stones above*	
6.15	Recumbent/slanting pentagon stone	2.0m L	criss-cross markings	2859 0733
▭	**Longstones**			
6.3	Recumbent/slanting longstone	3.9m L	paired with 6.4	2871 0702
6.6	Small slanting longstone	1.1m L	propped up; grouped	2868 0709

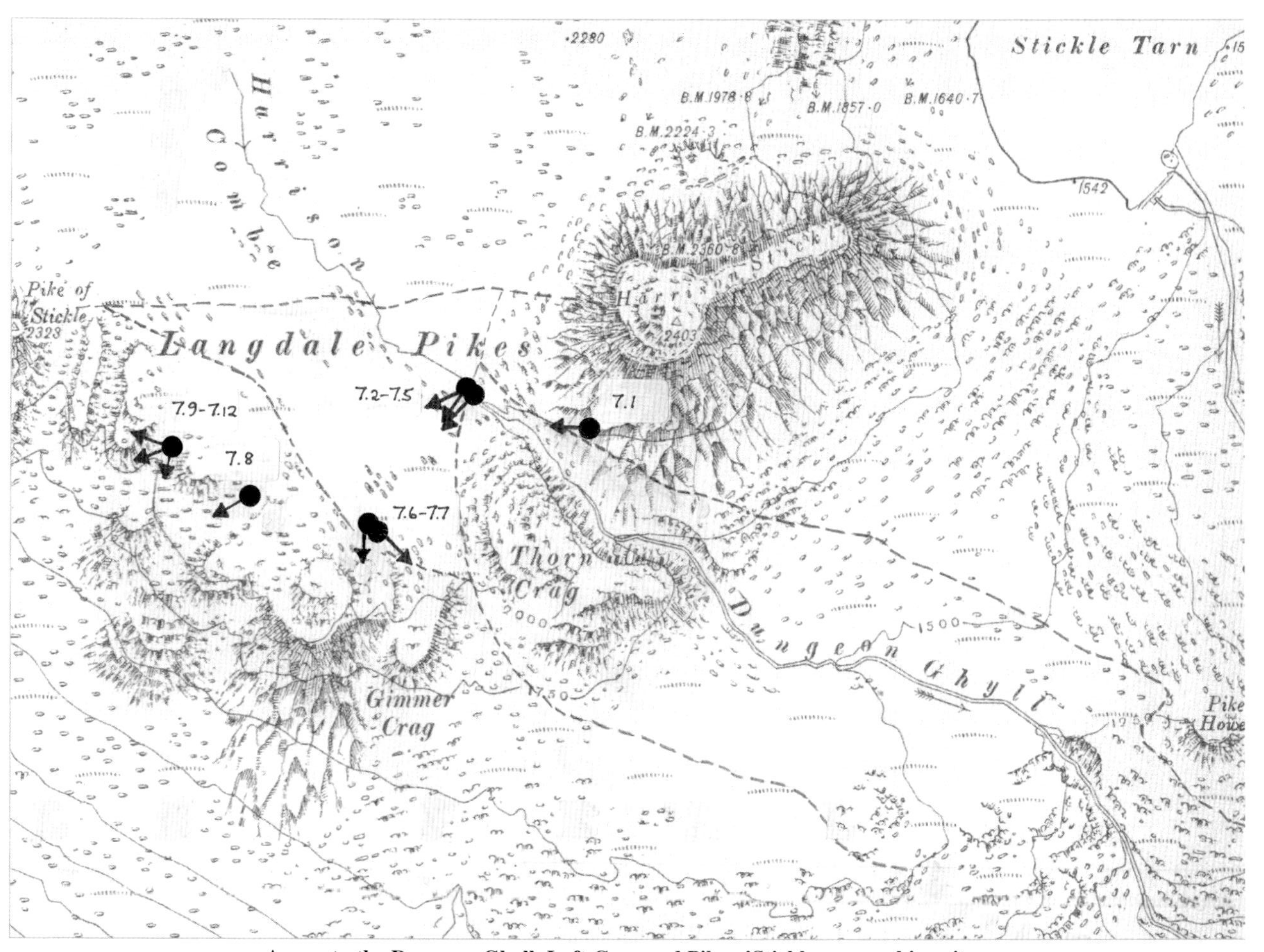

A way to the Dungeon Ghyll, Loft Crag and Pike o'Stickle axe working sites, showing locations and alignments of stones 7.1 – 7.12 (Chapter 7)

7 A WAY TO THE DUNGEON GHYLL, LOFT CRAG AND PIKE O' STICKLE AXE WORKING SITES

The Harrison Path

Several likely waymarks pointing NW in the Harrison Stickle direction, have already been noted. The way towards the Harrison path, indicated from the first of these – the longstone in the first cluster of stones described in Section 6 (6.3 above) – will now be picked up. In this chapter some potential waymarks close to the main axe stone sources are identified. Their presence here, on the approaches to the axe working sites, and pointing in relevant directions, could be highly significant.

The line from longstone 6.3 leads over the modern path from Pike Howe, which veers right along the ridge above the crags towards Stickle Tarn; and on to merge with the Harrison path. This continues on up past the western edge of Harrison Stickle in the direction of Harrison Combe, giving access to Pike o' Stickle - the stone source most heavily exploited for Neolithic axes.

Harrison Stickle now towers above to the right of the path ahead. Dungeon Ghyll and Thorn Crag lie to the left of Harrison Stickle.

On the way up the path, as it ascends the moorland apron below the crags of Harrison Stickle, several possible but modest recumbent waymarks may be noticed, suggesting a route across our path from the west towards Stickle Tarn. On the path itself, some small axe chipping sites have been identified, testifying to the Neolithic axe makers' presence in this vicinity [1].

Other large blocks visible off to the right, towards the foot of the Harrison Stickle crags include likely waymarks. For the moment these distractions will be ignored, and the way will be maintained up the present day Harrison path.

Towards the crags, the path climbs up more steeply between the deep upper ravine of Dungeon Ghyll on the left, and the high craggy side of Harrison Stickle on the right. The steep rock faces of Thorn Crag rise on the far side of the Dungeon Ghyll ravine.

Some screes stretching down below Harrison Stickle on the right provided one of the sources of the stone axes exploited by people forty-five centuries ago [2]. The ancient people chipped and picked the stone for axes here, with a magnificent southern panorama laid out below. The way SE down the valley to Lake Windermere and beyond is prominent. So too is the way southwards via Blea Tarn.

7.1 Upright/slanting lozenge block ⇒ WNW to Pike o' Stickle

A large, horizontally streaked block with a lozenge profile, becomes prominent, protruding upward on a little ledge at the foot of the Harrison Stickle outcrop above the path. Seen

7.1

A large *upright lozenge block* protrudes on a ledge at the foot of Harrison Stickle, pointing in a westerly direction. *NY 2813 0723*

A closer view shows the streaked face. The dome of Pike o' Stickle can be seen in the background, immediately to the left of the stone.

from the SE, it points slightly north of west past Pike o' Stickle over the longer upper point of its flattish, slightly wavy face; or west directly to Pike o' Stickle over its other upper point. More chipping sites occur in the scree to the west just beyond this last megalith [3].

From our approach up the Harrison path the block appears to be free standing. However, if examined from the other side below, it can be seen to be an upward outcropping rock feature. If it occurred naturally in this shape, its alignment is a curious coincidence. Perhaps the axe makers fashioned the outcrop so as to produce the guidestone effect.

Upper Dungeon Ghyll Crossing

The dome of Pike o' Stickle comes into view on the path in this vicinity. Our presence in the axe stone producing area is evident from the appearance of the blue Borrowdale tuff underfoot on the path. The path passes a high waterfall on Dungeon Ghyll below, and then flattens out into Harrison Combe. Working sites have been identified in the area of the path here [4]. Away to the left a ridge runs along from Loft Crag to Pike o' Stickle. Few rocks appear in the grassy moorland of the combe ahead.

7.2 Stepped lozenge profile block ⇒ SW to Loft Crag/Pike o' Stickle ridge

Now the steep sides of the Dungeon Ghyll ravine give way to gentle moorland slopes, making a crossing of the stream much easier. A junction path left leads across above the top of the Dungeon Ghyll ravine towards Loft Crag. A distinctive stepped stone sits at the far side of the stream crossing. Seen from a NE approach, it appears to point bluntly SW up to Loft Crag and the axe working site there. However, if viewed from a little round to the ENE, it gives a strong lozenge profile, and points the way WSW to the ridge between Loft Crag and Pike o' Stickle. Both directions lead to axe working sites.

7.3 Recumbent/slanting triangular stone ⇒ SW to Loft Crag

Sharp eyed observers will notice that this stone has another paired with it nearby. About 5m away on the near side of the stream a triangular stone, half embedded in the grass, protrudes and slants upwards, with a point in the Loft Crag direction, like the first alignment of the previous stepped stone.

7.4 Slanting triangular stone ⇒ SW to Loft Crag

This is not all. Only a little way downstream, sit a further close pair of slanting pointer stones. They bear a striking resemblance, on a smaller scale, to the pair below the third waterfall on Stickle Ghyll (5.3 and 5.4). Like the Stickle Ghyll pair, one triangular stone is accompanied by another longer pointed stone on its right side; and they are similarly positioned so as to be conspicuous from the path on the bank above. The lower stone, with a stepped, slanting back and a strong triangular profile, points to Loft Crag.

7.5 Slanting, elongated pentagonal block ⇒ SW to Pike o' Stickle ridge

The upper one, only about 2m away, displays in its slanting top a clear pentagonal profile

7.2
A *stepped block* by the Dungeon Ghyll crossing, shows a *lozenge profile,* and points SW. *NY 2792 0726*

7.3
A *slanting triangular stone* in the other edge of the stream points SW to Loft Crag. *NY 2792 0726*

7.4 and **7.5** In this pair a little downstream, a *slanting triangular stone*, points to Loft Crag, and a *pentagonal block* points to the ridge towards Pike o' Stickle. *NY 2792 0726*

7.4 and **7.5**
A closer view

with an upper point aligned to the ridge between Loft Crag and Pike o' Stickle. This way gives access to the axe working sites in the east and middle gullies; further pointers in this direction will be encountered shortly. Nearby to the south of this pair of stones, occur other axe working sites in the Dungeon Ghyll group [5].

Here, then, we have an important guidestone site indicating the way from the Harrison path to Loft Crag and Pike o' Stickle axe working sites. Two pairs of stones, conforming to typical shapes, situated at the earliest practicable crossing of Dungeon Ghyll above the ravine by Thorn Crag, indicate the way to the Loft Crag axe working site and the onward route to axe working sites in the gullies by Pike o' Stickle.

Loft Crag

7.6 Slanting lozenge block ⇒ south to Loft Crag

The junction path arrives below Loft Crag scree. A faint path bends round to the right below the crag. Near this path sits a large, slanting, lozenge shaped stone, showing diagonal streaks. It points just west of south towards the east of the crag top. Working sites have been identified in this direction - around the east, SE, south and NW of Loft Crag top [6].

7.7 Slanting lozenge sided block (streaked) ⇒ SE to Thorn Crag path

A few steps along the path that leads NW below the ridge to Pike o' Stickle, sits another interesting stone. If viewed from the west side, it presents the crude profile of a lozenge on its side. Its slanting face is extensively streaked, the streaks including a vein of quartz. It has a distinct SE side point – aligned along the way to the Thorn Crag path down to the valley.

Middle and East Gullies

A higher, more distinct path leads below the north side of Loft Crag westward, gradually rising towards a dip in the ridge between Loft Crag and Pike o' Stickle.

7.8 Recumbent pentagonal stone ⇒ WSW over ridge

Towards the dip a recumbent, low, rough topped stone, but with a well defined pentagonal shape, may be seen by the path on the right. It points WSW up over the ridge.

If this way is followed, it leads over the ridge and off to the left of the ridge path. The way down the other side to the east gully is passable, although the ground drops steeply. This way could have given access to axe chipping sites near to the top of the east gully (see 7.9 below).

7.9 Slanting triangular topped block ⇒ to Middle Gully

A short way from here along the ridge path towards Pike o' Stickle, a grassy dip appears below ahead. A gully - the east gully - drops down to the south. Several further axe working sites were identified by Claris and Quartermaine in this area [7].

7.6
A *slanting lozenge block* below Loft Crag is aligned just west of south, to the east side of Loft Crag top. *NY 2781 0718*

7.7
This *streaked, lozenge sided block* points the way SE past Thorn Crag to a downhill route. *NY 2781 0718*

From the ridge top approach, a group of no less than three possible stone waymarks attract attention, sitting spaced not far apart in the grass. The largest, on the south side, has a distinct chiselled triangular top, and on this approach from the east appears to point WNW down the edge of the ridge in the direction of the axe working sites in the next gully below.

7.10 Slanting pentagonal block ⇒ *WSW to Middle Gully*
The next stone in the trio, a little smaller, is a pentagonal style, slanting block pointing WSW – a line which also lies towards the middle gully.

7.11 Slanting diamond profile block ⇒ *west to Middle Gully*
The third, of similar size to the last, displays a diamond style profile and points slightly south of west – again giving access to the middle gully on the west side.

7.12 Lozenge/leaf arrowhead recumbent stone ⇒ *SSW down East Gully*
Before leaving this spot, a nice, flattish topped recumbent lozenge stone resembling an arrowhead may be noticed prone in the grass nearer the path. It points the way south to the east gully

These appear to be important indicators, marking the way to the east and middle gully axe working sites. If the path is followed along the ridge top towards Pike o' Stickle, another dip is reached before the final rise overlooking the Pike o' Stickle south scree. This last dip occurs at the top of the middle gully; but stones near the top of the gully do not display any obvious waymark characteristics.

Pike o' Stickle

It is now an easy few steps along the ridge to the top of Pike o' Stickle. Immediately before the craggy Pike o' Stickle dome, the substantial south scree runs from the very top of the ridge far down the fellside. The buttresses beside the scree provided a particularly productive source of stone axes [8], which were distributed the length and breadth of the country.

The south scree has proved rich in remains of axe making activity, and could have been approached from above from the spot now reached, to gain access to the axe making material. The sides of Pike o' Stickle dome rise sheer up from towards the top of the scree, making access to axe making sites on the actual buttresses almost impossible from there. Access could have been gained a little way down the scree, past the cave on the Pike o' Stickle east side, up natural ledges rising from the scree. The ancient axe makers could also have approached the buttresses, from which much of the stone was chipped away, by an approach immediately beyond the top of the south scree, on ledges around the east side of the dome. Alternatively, if they went round the back of the dome the buttresses could more easily be approached from the NW side.

7.8

A *recumbent pentagonal stone* points WSW diagonally over the Pike o' Stickle ridge to the axe working sites in the gullies nearby. *NY 2768 0723*

7.9, 7.10 and **7.11**

A *trio of stones* become conspicuous in a dip on the Loft Crag to Pike o' Stickle ridge. All suggest the way to the Middle Gully axe working site down the ridge WNW. *NY 2759 0728*

At intervals from the Great Langdale valley at Millbeck, apparent megalithic waymarks have guided us across the Stickle Ghyll waterfalls, over the Pike Howe ridge and across upper Dungeon Ghyll all the way to the principal stone axe working sites. From here onward, significant signs begin to appear of a way from the north – but exploration of that route must await another publication.

7.12
This *lozenge/leaf arrowhead recumbent stone* on the ridge points the way just west of south to the East Gully. *NY 2759 0728*

This approach along the ridge from Loft Crag gives a fine view of the Pike o' Stickle dome.

Table 7a

Guidestones, and directions pointed in Chapter 7

Guide stone no.	Type	Align-ment	Situation	Guide stone rating
⇒	**Pointers to the Loft Crag Site**			
7.2	Lozenge profile stepped block	215°	Dungeon Ghyll crossing	***
7.3	Recumbent/slanting triangular stone	215°	Dungeon Ghyll crossing	**
7.4	Slanting triangular stone	225°	Dungeon Ghyll crossing	***
7.6	Slanting lozenge block	185°	path below Loft Crag	*
⇒	**Pointers to the gully sites**			
7.2	Upright stepped lozenge block	245°	Dungeon Ghyll crossing	***
7.5	Slanting pentagonal block	235°	Dungeon Ghyll crossing	***
7.8	Recumbent pentagonal stone	245°	Loft Crag/Pike o' Stickle ridge	*
7.9	Slanting triangular topped block	285°	Loft Crag/Pike o' Stickle ridge	***
7.10	Slanting pentagonal block	250°	Loft Crag/Pike o' Stickle ridge	**
7.11	Slanting diamond block	265°	Loft Crag/Pike o' Stickle ridge	**
7.12	Recumbent lozenge stone	190°	Loft Crag/Pike o' Stickle ridge	*
⇒	**Pointer to Pike o' Stickle**			
7.1	Upright/slanting streaked lozenge block	270°	edge of Harrison Stickle	***
⇒	**Pointer down the valley**			
7.7	Slanting streaked lozenge sided block	135°	path below Loft Crag	**

Summary: A way to the Dungeon Ghyll, Loft Crag and Pike o' Stickle axe working sites

Locations
The stones described in this chapter are not in general the most striking examples that we have encountered – perhaps because at this height, near the summit of the Pikes, suitable large rocks were in short supply. However, a special feature of the stones identified in this chapter, is that they all sit within the vicinity of actual stone axe working sites; and all except one *actually point towards known chipping sites*. (The exception is one below Loft Crag, which points the way back down a natural way – the Thorn Crag path.)

The megaliths which carry the most conviction as potential waymarks are the two pairs of stones of characteristic shape situated at a natural crossing of Dungeon Ghyll. This lies above the top of the falls, at the entrance to Harrison Combe - the strategic crossing for anyone coming up the Harrison path. A path crosses here at the present day. Axe chipping sites have been identified not far from this crossing on both sides of the stream.

Directions indicated (Table 7a)
Apparent megalithic markers have provided strong evidence of a way across above the top of Dungeon Ghyll ravine, to the Loft Crag and Pike o' Stickle axe working sites. They have pointed the way to the main stone axe working sites along the ridge above Mickleden – Loft Crag, east gully, middle gully, and Pike o' Stickle, as follows.

To the Loft Crag axe working site
At least three of the stones at the Dungeon Ghyll crossing, two of them with 'probable' ratings, could be interpreted as pointing the way to the Loft Crag chipping sites: the stepped lozenge block (7.2); recumbent triangular stone (7.3) and slanting triangular stone (7.4). A lozenge block below Loft Crag may possibly point this way (7.6).

To East and Middle Gully chipping sites
Evidence of axe stone working has also been found in the middle and east gullies, below the ridge between Loft Crag and Pike o' Stickle. Several stones, some with three star ratings, indicate the way in this direction.

At the Dungeon Ghyll crossing, the stepped lozenge stone (7.2) can be interpreted as pointing this way; and the slanting elongated pentagon stone here (7.5) points in this direction. The tentative recumbent pentagon NW of Loft Crag (7.8) points over the ridge towards the gullies. The trio of markers point to the middle gully (7.9, 7.10, 7.11). A recumbent leaf arrowhead on the ridge (7.12) points to the east gully.

To Pike o' Stickle site
7.1 One large megalith has been identified pointing direct from the top of Dungeon Ghyll to Pike o' Stickle – the main axe working area. This is the prominent lozenge block protruding up from a ledge above the Dungeon Ghyll ravine, at the entrance to Harrison Combe, and marking the way to Pike o' Stickle.

The author has not identified any stones on the ridge from Loft Crag to Pike o' Stickle pointing the way to Pike o' Stickle. This may at first be regarded as curious. However, several possible reasons could be advanced for this. Firstly, the dome of Pike o' Stickle is clearly visible as a foresight from the top of Dungeon Ghyll onwards, and would in itself provide a foresight. Secondly, it is possible that the traditional route to Pike o' Stickle lay as pointed by the stones, via Loft Crag and the tops of the gullies and not direct in a straight line to the dome. Moreover, the stones on the ridge apparently marking ways down to the gullies could suggest that access to the main stone source on the buttresses of Pike o' Stickle was gained by descending the gullies and crossing the south scree a little way down, where the steep eastern rock side of Pike o' Stickle gives way to slightly more accessible rocks.

To Loft Crag/Thorn Crag path SE down the valley

One stone has pointed a new route away from the axe working sites. The slanting, streaked lozenge below Loft Crag marks the way SE down the Thorn Crag path (7.7).

Stone types and groups (Table 7b)

No standing stones have been revealed in this part of our exploration. Three *triangular* stones have been identified. Two of these have occurred in upper Dungeon Ghyll – a slanting topped triangular block (7.3) and the slanting stepped block with a triangular profile (7.4). Then on the ridge towards Pike o' Stickle, a stone with a triangular, chisel ended top pointed down to the gullies (7.9).

No less than six of the potential waymarks have displayed a *lozenge* shape. The large megalith on the ledge at the end of Harrison Stickle shows a pronounced lozenge profile and top face (7.1). The first stone described in upper Dungeon Ghyll displays a stepped lozenge profile (7.2). The first of the stones below Loft Crag showed a crude lozenge profile (7.6), and the second here a smooth slanting lozenge side (7.7). One of the trio of stones on the ridge displays a slanting, diamond style profile (7.11). The last stone described is a prone lozenge in the shape of a leaf arrowhead (7.12).

The *pentagonal* shape has occurred three times. One of the stones in upper Dungeon Ghyll presents an elongated pentagonal shape (7.5). A recumbent example appears on the ridge (7.8). One of the final trio of stones also shows a slanting pentagonal shape (7.10).

The characteristic of *streaked surfaces* has recurred three times – once in the large lozenge at the edge of Harrison Stickle (7.1); again in the first lozenge below Loft Crag (7.6) and conspicuously again in the second smooth faced lozenge there (7.7).

The *pairing* of stones has been a striking feature at the Dungeon Ghyll crossing. One pair (7.4 and 7.5) display shapes similar to those of a larger pair at the Stickle Ghyll waterfall crossing – a slanting triangle closely accompanied by an elongated pointed stone. A *trio* of stones has occurred on the ridge above the gullies (7.9, 7.10 and 7.11).

Table 7b

Stone types and features – Chapter 7

Stone no.	Type	Size	Features	Map ref. (NY)
	Standing Stones			
	None			
	Triangular Stones			
7.3	Slanting triangular stone	0.7m H	paired with 7.2	2792 0726
7.4	Upright/slanting triangular stone	0.8m H	paired with 7.5	2792 0726
7.9	Upright triangular top block	1.4m L	grouped with 7.10/7.11	2759 0728
	Lozenge Stones			
7.1	Upright lozenge block	1.8m H	prominent; streaked	2813 0723
7.2	Upright stepped lozenge block	0.9m H	paired with 7.3	2792 0726
7.6	Upright/slanting lozenge block	1.2m H	streaked	2781 0717
7.7	Upright lozenge sided block	1.7m W	streaked	2781 0718
7.11	Slanting diamond block	tbc	grouped with 7.9, 7.10	2759 0728
7.12	Recumbent lozenge block	1.1m L	arrowhead style	2759 0728
	Pentagonal Stones			
7.5	Upright/slanting pentagonal block	1.0m H	paired with 7.4	2792 0726
7.8	Recumbent pentagonal stone	1.6m L		2768 0723
7.10	Slanting pentagonal block	1.2m L	grouped with 7.9/7.11	2759 0728

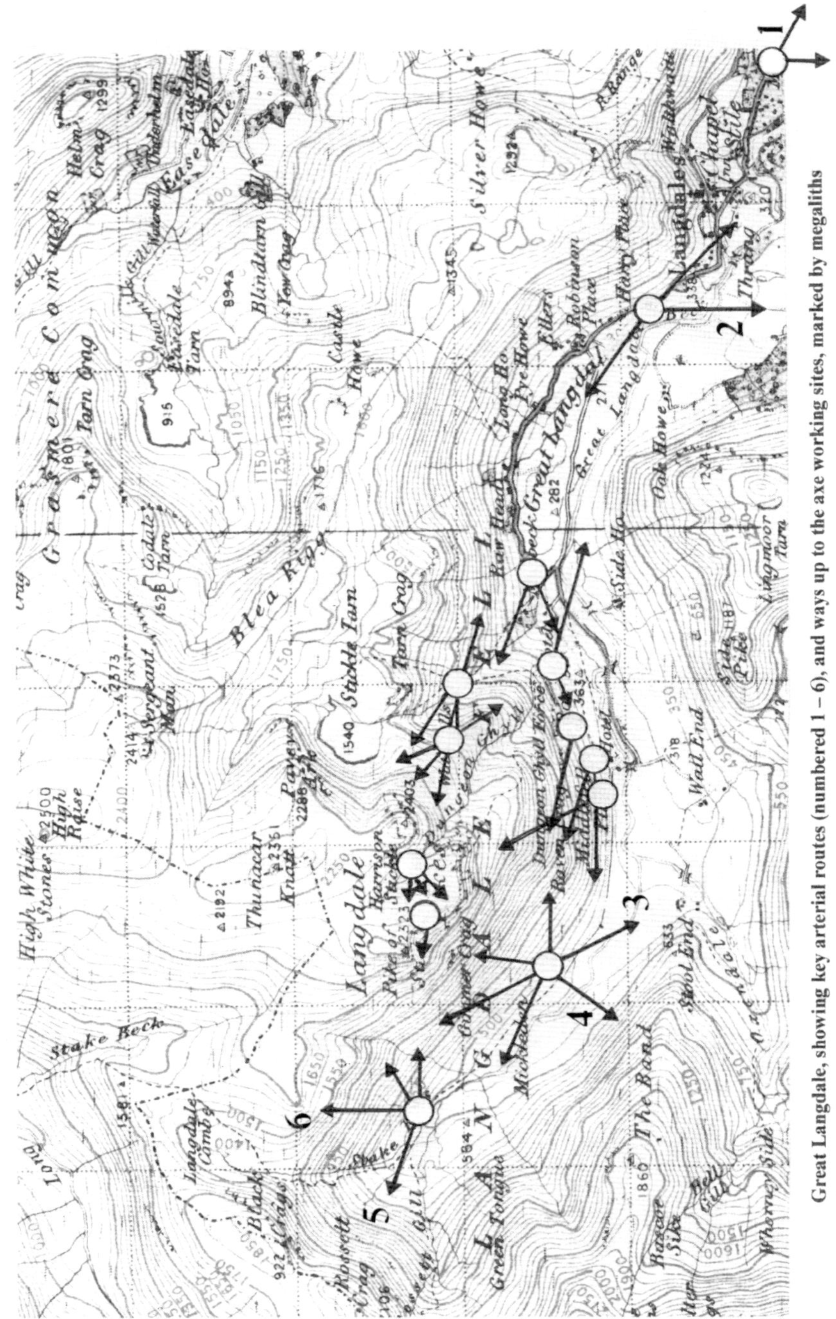

Great Langdale, showing key arterial routes (numbered 1 – 6), and ways up to the axe working sites, marked by megaliths

8 CONCLUSION

Ways marked by megaliths

The starting point of this book was the assumption, shared generally by archaeological authorities, that a Neolithic route lay along Great Langdale to and from the axe 'factories'. Considerable prima facie evidence has been presented, to suggest that megaliths were used by the Neolithic people to mark a way up and down the valley. Likely pointers on the arterial route along the valley have been traced from a standing stone on Elterwater Common, past Pike o' Stickle, to a standing pentagon and associated stones at the head of the valley. Junction pointers have also been identified, suggesting other significant arterial axe distribution routes leading away from the axe making sites.

A number of megaliths have been identified which point ways up the fellsides to the high axe making sites around the tops of the Pikes. Ways have been identified, with the help of megaliths, from Millbeck via the Stickle Ghyll waterfalls to the Pike Howe ridge and Stickle Tarn; and to the Harrison Stickle, Loft Crag and Pike o' Stickle axe working sites.

In Chapter 2, potential guidestones in the form of standing stones, triangular, lozenge, pentagonal and long stones were identified at the mouth of the Great Langdale valley. Finds of rough out axes at Loughrigg Tarn and High Close confirm that the Neolithic stone axe workers passed this way. Several potential waymark stones were identified around the important rock art site at the Langdale Boulders, which is thought to date to the Late Neolithic/Early Bronze Age. This association suggests – although it does not conclusively prove – that the stones could have been set up there in that era.

There is remarkable consistency in the directions pointed by the megaliths identified in this chapter. Some point the way down the River Brathay valley towards the head of Lake Windermere: a natural communication route leading on to Lancashire and Yorkshire. Several more point south to another natural route, followed today by the A 593, via Oxen Fell and Yew Tree Tarn to the head of Coniston Water. This would give access to the Neolithic settlements in the south of Cumbria. Some further megaliths already begin to point ways up towards the axe chipping sites in the Pikes.

Some dramatic megalithic specimens in Chapter 3, including two good standing stones, continue to point directions up and down the Great Langdale valley. Several more stones now point ways diagonally up the hillside in the direction of stone axe making sites. Potential guidestones are repeatedly positioned by watercourses, or on brows and hillocks. A long established bridleway along the foot of the hillside, but above the valley floor, passes by these stones.

Chapter 4 reveals further dramatic pentagonal and triangular megalithic specimens, apparently pointing ways up to the axe stone bearing ridge for those coming from the

SW; and ways setting out in the opposite direction. Stones repeatedly point in the direction of several natural arterial routes from the foot of Pike o' Stickle – especially via Wrynose Pass to the south west; Rossett Hause and Sty Head to the west; and Stake Pass to Borrowdale and the north. These are all routes followed by present day footpaths. They would provide the obvious routes for Neolithic people taking their axe rough outs and flocks of animals back to the lowlands on the periphery of the Lake District. The routes correlate with those assumed by archaeologists like Clare Fell.

In Chapter 5, crossing points over the striking natural feature of the Stickle Ghyll waterfalls were explored. Apparent guidestones were noted beside the stream; in the actual stream bed itself, and on the tops of waterfalls. A number of stones point ways up the east fellside of the Pike Howe ridge in the direction of stone axe working sites at Stickle Tarn and Harrison Stickle. This fellside provides an easy, grassy way up to the Pikes, particularly suitable if flocks of animals were to be herded up for summer grazing. Other stones point the way back down the valley.

An intriguing feature of Chapter 6 is the megalithic indicators now pointing directly towards stone axe chipping sites at Stickle Tarn, Harrison Stickle East and Harrison Stickle West from nearby on a natural way below the east brow of the ridge. Some stones again point ways back down the fellside.

The most prominent features in Chapter 7 were the two pairs of stream crossing markers on Dungeon Ghyll, at the lip of Harrison Combe above the uppermost waterfall. They point the way up to axe chipping sites at Loft Crag and at the Gullies between Loft Crag and Pike o' Stickle. On the ridge itself, possible guidestones point down to the gully axe chipping sites.

Characteristics of the stones identified

Shapes

The blocks and slabs which have been identified, are of types consistent with those found in the great stone circles of Cumbria. Stones have been large and small; standing, slanting and recumbent, as in stone circles: such features have not been the decisive factors in identifying them as possible waymarks. The first defining characteristic has been shape – their shapes in profile, or the shapes of their upper surfaces.

Four shapes in particular have predominated. Triangular, lozenge/diamond, pentagonal, and longstone shapes occur frequently in the profiles of the stones; or in the outlines of their upper surfaces, which in many cases slant up to a point offering a directional indication.

The shapes of the stones which have been identified sometimes seem to reflect those to be found in the arrowheads and spearheads used at the time; and - in the case of diamonds - a shape also displayed in contemporary prehistoric art.

Stones have been encountered with profiles that are pointed at the top or the side; and also top surfaces with pointed triangular, diamond and pentagonal shapes. Sometimes stones exhibit different pointed surfaces or profiles, when viewed from different standpoints, suggesting routes in two directions. This effect could have been achieved deliberately by the Neolithic people - just as in modern times, signposts are often used to indicate ways in more than one direction. Sometimes a stone has a slightly turned top point and this may signify a bending route.

From time to time natural streaks in the faces of the stones draw attention to them as likely guidestones.

Groupings

Whilst a number of possible guidestones appear singly, the repeated occurrence of such stones in *pairs* has been a notable feature. Stones in pairs may be positioned close together, or spaced apart. Several examples have been noted of "mother and baby" close waymark pairs – a large pointer stone closely accompanied by a relatively small one. Occasionally, but less commonly, possible waymarks have occurred in clusters of three or more.

Locations

Relative prominence in the landscape has been another key characteristic. The large size of some of the stones described does on its own make them the most prominent in the vicinity. However, stones large and small are often given prominence by apparently deliberate strategic positioning. They are associated with three types of natural feature in particular. Stones are frequently located near the crossing of *water courses;* in actual stream beds, or on or near waterfalls. Likely waymarks have been identified at several of the major stream crossings on the NE side up the Great Langdale valley – Millbeck, Dungeon Ghyll, Grave Gill, Troughton Beck. This feature has occurred again at the crossing of upper Dungeon Ghyll, at the entrance to Harrison Combe. Apparent guidestones have occurred on or in the vicinity of several of the spectacular waterfalls on Stickle Ghyll.

Possible guidestones are often placed at the foot of a *hillock*; or on the side of a hillock below the brow. Kirk Howe, and the three Scots Pines provided good examples along the valley. Such stones are also found placed near (usually below) other prominent *natural rock features*, such as distinctive rock outcrops, large rocks or cloven stones. This has been seen at the Langdale Boulders and at the three Scots Pines below Raven Crag; and particularly in the occurrence of likely waymarks at successive rock outcrops below the ridge top on the SE side of Pike Howe ridge

Alignments

It is important to understand that this thesis does *not* suggest that the megaliths in Great Langdale exhibit the characteristics of stones set up in alignment with one another in *rows* or *avenues*, like those identified by Aubrey Burl. Nor does it rest on the idea of *ley lines* or *long distance foresights.* The megaliths in Great Langdale are typically situated at intervals, near prominent natural features, their significance lying, as waymarks, in the directions they point, not in any multiple alignments with one another in straight rows.

Routes indicated

The map at the beginning of this chapter (page 120) summarises the main lines of the way apparently marked up Great Langdale; ways marked to the axe making sites; and the beginnings of major arterial routes. The main routes identified are as follows.

Valley route

The likely route of the Neolithic way up Great Langdale has been traced along the NE side of the valley. The majority of the stones identified, lie along the lower slopes of the fellside above the valley floor, suggesting that this was the preferred level for a Neolithic way along the valley. This is consistent with the characteristics of key Neolithic routes identified elsewhere. Interestingly, much of this route is followed today at this level by the B 5343 from Elterwater Common to Millbeck; and then by the bridleway from the Great Langdale car park to the head of Great Langdale.

Key waymark points are as follows:

Elterwater Common
Rock art site
Millbeck crossing
Dungeon Ghyll crossing
Kirk Howe
foot of Raven Crag
Grave Gill crossing
foot of Pike o' Stickle
Troughton Beck crossing
foot of Martcrag.

Routes up to the axe working sites

Ways up to the axe chipping sites are repeatedly suggested by megalithic pointers. Strong indications of a route from Stickle Ghyll falls up to the Pike Howe ridge and then on to the NW edge of Stickle Tarn have been identified, suggesting that Stickle Tarn may have been a focal point for the axe stone workers, for setting up camp. A major route up to the axe workings via Stickle Ghyll waterfalls, Pike Howe ridge, the apron of Harrison Stickle, Dungeon Ghyll and Loft Crag has been described, leading right up to the gullies to the south of Pike o' Stickle dome. Ways back down the valley SE are also marked, and across the valley southward in the Blea Tarn direction.

The starts of several other routes up to the axe working sites have been identified:

North up Kirk Howe and Pike Howe
NW from the foot of Raven Crag up the Gimmer Crag path
NNW from Mickleden up Troughton Beck
North to Mart Crag and Stake Pass.

Even today footpaths follow most of the routes indicated – for example from Millbeck to Stickle Ghyll waterfalls; and along the edge of the Pike Howe ridge to Stickle Tarn. In particular, megaliths point to the Harrison path up by Dungeon Ghyll to the Loft Crag and Pike o' Stickle axe working sites. This fits with the findings by Claris and Quartermaine of evidence of axe working activity on the Harrison path.

Arterial routes

The main arterial routes which have been suggested by megaliths identified in the previous chapters, are numbered from 1 to 6 on the map on page 120. These routes may be summarized as follows.

1 ESE to Yorkshire

Standing stones at Elterwater Common and the Great Langdale rock art site point the continuing main Great Langdale way ESE, down the valley towards the head of Lake Windermere. This gives access by boat down Lake Windermere; or onwards via Kendal, Kirkby Lonsdale and the Aire gap, or by Sedburgh and Wensleydale, into Yorkshire.

2 and 3 Coniston, Furness and the south

Ways south towards Coniston, indicated by megaliths at both Elterwater Common and the Langdale Boulders (2), would lead on to important Neolithic settlements in the Furness area; with the likelihood of onward transmission of the stone axes by boat down the coast southwards. Likely guidestones indicate ways from the axe workings in the Langdale Fell area SE to Little Langdale (3), which would provide another onward route to Coniston and Furness.

4 Wrynose Pass and the SW

Possible waymarks suggest a way SSW from the area below Raven Crag towards Wrynose Pass; and also SSW from Langdale Fell over the foot of The Band, towards Wrynose Pass. These ways would lead on to routes to the west coast via Eskdale, and the SW coast via Dunnerdale.

5 Rossett Hause and the west

From Mickleden, apparent guidestones point a continuing way WNW towards Rossett Gill, gives access via Angle Tarn and Esk Hause to the west.

6 Stake Pass, Borrowdale and the north

In Mickleden, stones mark an onward route northwards up the hillside past Pike o' Stickle, leading to Stake Pass and the way north to Borrowdale.

The routes suggested by the stones, as outlined above, match to a large extent with those inferred by archaeologists for the distribution of stone axes from Great Langdale.

Some issues considered

In these pages, empirical evidence of a series of distinctive megaliths in the Great Langdale valley, and up the fellsides to the axe workings in the Pikes, has been presented, and the hypothesis of Neolithic routes has been put forward to explain them. Some obvious issues arise from this preliminary exploration; examples are as follows.

Why would Neolithic people choose to mark their trackways with megaliths?

It might be suggested that the Neolithic people wouldn't need, or want, to mark the way with great stones, as described in this text – that well worn paths would be established, and the way would be familiar.

This issue needs to be considered in relation to the features of the landscape as it is thought to have existed in those far off days; and the nature of the axe manufacturing and distribution process. We do know that none of the landmarks which have been imposed on the landscape by the people of historic times, then existed. The valley bottoms are likely to have been densely wooded. This could have made finding the way more difficult. Parts of the valley sides would also have been wooded, perhaps up to a level as high as 500m. This would have reduced the visibility of natural landmarks such as the Pikes themselves [1].

Axe making in Great Langdale is thought to have been a summer seasonal activity [2]. In the early centuries it appears that people came from the coastal lowlands to chip out the rough axes on Langdale Fell. Later – at the peak of production – people from more distant parts obtained access to the finished products. If people from Yorkshire, or from intermediate areas between Great Langdale and Yorkshire, travelled to Great Langdale to manufacture or obtain axes, they had to find their way through an environment away from home. The ravages of the elements could have rendered paths indistinct over the winter season. Over some types of terrain it is likely that no clear path was worn down at all. In short, it is by no means certain that the way from the east up Great Langdale would have been familiar or self evident. Megalithic waymarks *could* have performed a valuable function in marking the way.

Even today, where there are so many familiar landmarks in the modern environment, we take great pains to signpost each and every road junction. We do not say that, because many people know the way, it is unnecessary to put up signposts.

The issue "Why?" needs also to be addressed in terms of cultural values and symbolism. Unfortunately few firm facts are known to illuminate this context. However, the knowledge that we do have offers support for the interpretation of megaliths developed in these pages – both at functional and symbolic levels. We do not and cannot know the mindset of the people who travelled Cumbrian Lakeland 4,500 years ago. They lived a different way of life. What we do know is that they excelled in working with stone - from the making of artifacts as small as arrowheads, to the erection of huge dolmens, tombs and stone circles. The scale of these monuments strongly suggests that, in addition to whatever function they performed, they held an important symbolic or spiritual significance – which we do not now fully understand. For example, there was no functional necessity to heave up colossal capstones found on many dolmens – this was something that was done in accordance with the customs and beliefs of the time. Similarly, evidence has been put forward here that the Neolithic people laboured to position megalithic waymarks in Great Langdale, that might seem to some today to be out of proportion to any purely practical requirement for signposting. This does not mean that they cannot have been waymarks – but merely that we do not know or understand the full significance which may have been attached to them, within the values of the people of that distant period of prehistory.

What scientific proof is there to show any human involvement in the positioning or shaping of the stones identified in the Neolithic period?

Archaeologists identify and date many artefacts – including sculptures and stonework from – say – the Roman, Saxon, or Norman periods – by shape. The same method has been applied in these pages. The evidence of megalithic markers presented here consists of the identification of stones of shape types used by prehistoric people in the creation of stone circles of the Late Neolithic/Early Bronze Age; together with certain locational characteristics.

Additionally, a number of standing stones or slabs have been identified. The laws of gravity suggest that they are unlikely to have arrived in such a position naturally; and that somebody erected them. Other megaliths have been shown to have been propped up at one end so as to produce an upper surface slanting up to a point, which suggests the work of human hands.

To make allowances for the variable strength of the empirical evidence for the identification of stones as megalithic waymarks, a star rating scheme has been applied as described at the end of the first chapter. This enables differentiation between those stones having features strongly indicative of waymarks, and others that are more tentative. The author has relied primarily on those stones achieving a rating of three stars or more in indicating likely Neolithic routes.

It is acknowledged that the thesis remains to be scientifically proven. This does not mean that it is not correct - any more than the scientifically unproven but widely accepted thesis that smoking causes cancer. In archaeological terms, the thesis may be compared to the generally accepted - but scientifically unproven - proposition that the evidence of a decline in tree pollens in certain areas of Cumbria in prehistoric times was caused by the Neolithic people clearing trees. There is no scientific proof that Neolithic or any other human intervention led to this decline; but orthodox interpretation accepts a connection.

Standing stones and other megaliths are notoriously difficult to date. In the case of the megaliths described in these pages, it is possible that studies applying modern scientific archaeological techniques might reveal any signs of human intervention in the shaping and positioning of the megaliths described. For example, analysis of the undersurfaces, and the sockets or seats of the megaliths, might reveal how long they have been located in their present positions, and any evidence of Neolithic or other human involvement in their shaping or placement.

Surely the alignments of the stones described could have occurred purely by chance? Are they not merely erratics rather than waymarks?

It may be suggested that if *any* area of landscape which contained a scatter of boulders was chosen, the random occurrence of different shapes, sizes and alignments would be likely to offer the possibility of some common alignments.

The criteria that have been applied in the identification of megaliths should be borne in mind in considering the idea that such megaliths could have occurred at random. Firstly, the shapes of the stones have been a defining characteristic. Secondly, positioning in the landscape has been such as to draw attention to the particular megaliths identified. Often the stones are the largest in the vicinity. In other cases, if not of large size, they are positioned near a natural feature which draws attention to them. Thirdly, evidence of human intervention exists in relation to a number of the megaliths described – stones that have been erected upright, or propped up at a slant.

The author has explored many a rocky lower hillside which has *not* revealed conspicuous stones with triangular, lozenge or pentagonal shapes, and upper surfaces rising to a point, linked in series to suggest a trackway. However, further systematic survey work, applying the defining characteristics of waymarks as described in these pages, could be useful to check that such stones can not be found to occur at random in the wider landscape.

The alternative random hypothesis – that the megaliths identified in this text occurred naturally and without human intervention – itself faces a number of difficulties. The repeated occurrence of stones of certain shapes, with points consistently indicating significant directions, has to be explained away; and the correspondence of those alignments with known Neolithic routes. Similarly the repeated occurrence of standing stones with points aligned in significant directions, has to be explained. On the balance of probabilities, it seems more likely that all these features provide an indication of deliberate waymarking of a known route by people of late Neolithic times.

Wider implications

A new hypothesis in relation to megaliths in Great Langdale has been presented in these pages. It *is* a hypothesis: whilst extensive empirical evidence has been advanced, human intervention in the choice and positioning of the stones remains to be scientifically proved. Indeed, this study might best be described as a preliminary reconnaissance, rather than a conclusive survey. Only the most prominent and accessible stones have been described at this stage. Nevertheless, the cumulative evidence of all the stones described, strongly supports the working hypothesis that megaliths with certain characteristics were used by the Neolithic people as signs in stone - whether functional or symbolic – for their communication routes; and that their routes up Great Langdale, and up to the axe working sites, can still be identified today by reference to such waymarks.

The recognition of the shapes and directional indications in the stones described, requires a degree of spatial aptitude and familiarity, which may well have been better developed in many of the Neolithic people used to the ancient landscape, than amongst some of us today.

Only one initial sample route has been presented here; the author has identified many other stones suggesting similar waymarked routes across Cumbria. Further ways up to the axe working sites have been identified; and long stretches of arterial routes. Signs of possible megalithic waymarks have been observed in Wales, the West Country, Scotland, and Northern Ireland.

The discovery of megaliths with the features described above, apparently performing the function of waymarks in the Late Neolithic/Early Bronze Age, is of major importance. The identification of such potential megalithic waymarks offers the possibility that our knowledge of Neolithic communication routes could be greatly enlarged, and that Neolithic route maps might be drawn for some parts of Britain and beyond. The discovery of such ways could lead to a better understanding of Neolithic communications and the interrelationships of Neolithic sites; and offer the potential for the discovery of further axe working sites and other Neolithic sites.

REFERENCES

CHAPTER 1

1 Fell, C	1950	The Great Langdale stone-axe factory TCWAAS NS L p 7; and
Plint, R.G.	1962	Stone Axe Factory Sites in the Cumbrian Fells TCWAAS NS LXII p 19; and
Manby, T.	1965	The Distribution of rough out, Cumbrian and related stone axes of Lake District origin in Northern England TSWAAS NS LXV pp 1-37
2 Bradley, R. and Edmonds,M.	1993	Interpreting the Axe Trade: Production and exchange in Neolithic Britain. Cambridge University Press Ch 10
3 Pennington,W	1970	Vegetation History in the North-West of England: a Regional Synthesis, in Studies in the Vegetational History of the British Isles (eds. D. Walker & R.G. West). Cambridge pp 41- 79
	1975	The effect of Neolithic man on the environment in north-west England: the use of absolute pollen diagrams. In J.G. Evans, S. Limbrey and H. Cleere (eds), The Effect of Man on th Landscape: The Hilghland Zone, pp74-86. London: Council for British Archaeology, Research Report 11.
4 Bradley, R. and Edmonds, M.		op. cit p 139
5 ibid.		Ch 6
6 Clough,T.H.McK		1973 Excavations on a Langdale axe chipping site in 1969 and 1970. TCWAAS NS LXXIII p 30
7 Bradley, R and Edmonds, M		op. cit
8 ibid.		p 138 & p 158
9 ibid.		Ch 9
10 Clough		op.cit. p 39
11 Bradley, R and Edmonds, M		op. cit p 199
12 Claris, P and Quartermaine, J	1989	The Neolithic Quarries and Axe Factory Sites of Great Langdale and Scafell Pike. A New Field Survey. PPS 55 pp 1-25
13 Cummins, W A	1979	Neolithic stone axes: distribution and trade in England and Wales. In CBA Research Report No 23 pp 5-12; and
Cummins, W A	1980	Stone Axes as a Guide to Neolithic Communications and Boundaries in England and Wales PPS 46 pp 45-60 (p59)
14 Bradley, R and Edmonds, M		op. cit p 48
15 Cummins, W.A	1979	Neolithic stone axes: distribution and trade in England and Wales. In CBA Research Report No 23, p 10
16 Muir, R and Welfare, H	1983	The National Trust Guide to Prehistoric and Roman Britain. George Philip, pp 55-56
17 Stone, J.F.S. and Wallis, F.S.	1951	The Third Report…on the Petrological Determination of Stone Axes PPS 17 p 118
18 Robert Gardiner ed.	1996	Conway's History of the Ship: The Earliest Ships Conway Maritime Press pp 11-18
19	1929	TCWAAS NS XXIX p 331
20		PSAL 2 vi p 438 (Loughrigg Tarn)

	Author	Year	Reference
21	Cowper, H.S.	1901	TCWAAS NS I p 135 (Hird Wood - Troutbeck)
	Plint, R.G.	1960	TCWAAS LX p 200 (Underscar)
	Plint, R.G.	1962	TCWAAS NS LXII p 20 (Slyne)
	Fell, C.	1950	TCWAAS NS L p 10 (Morecambe)
22	Davies	1963	TCWAAS NS LXIII pp 53-54 (Thorpe Fell)
	Manby, T.G.	1965	TCWAAS NS LXV p26
23	Burl, A	1976	The Stone Circles of the British Isles Yale University Press
24	Cooper, H S	1934	TCWAAS NS XXXIV p 91
25	Waterhouse, J.	1985	1985 The Stone Circles of Cumbria Phillimore pp 87-88
26	Foster, E	1913	The Icknield Way. Constable
27	Belloc, H	1935	The Old Road. Constable
28	Claris, P and Quartermaine, J		op. cit. p 19
29	ibid.		p 6
30	Fell, C	1950	The Great Langdale stone-axe factory TCWAAS NS L p 10
31	Fell, C	1964	The Cumbrian type of Polished Stone Axe and its Distribution in Britain PPS 30 pp 41-44
32	Manby, T	1965	The Distribution of rough out, Cumbrian and related stone axes of Lake District origin in Northern England TCWAAS NS LXV
33	Cummins, W.A	1979	Neolithic stone axes: distribution and trade in England and Wales. In CBA Research Report No 23, p 10
34	Taylor, M.W	1886	The Prehistoric Remains on Moordivock, near Ullswater. TCWAAS OS VIII, p 342
35	James, D.J.	1978-9	The Prehistoric standing stones of Breconshire. In Brycheiniog XVIII, pp 18 - 20; and
	Bird, A.J	1972	The Menhir in Cardiganshire: A Re-assessment. In Ceredigion (7) p 46
36	Burl, A	1976	op. cit pp 267-8
37	Bowen, E.G. and Gresham, C.A.	1967	History of Merioneth. I Dolgelly (p 57) , quoted in Burl, A op.cit pp 257-8
38	Burl, A	1993	From Carnac to Callanish Yale University Press p5
39	Burl, A	1976	The Stone Circles of the British Isles Yale University Press pp 57-60

CHAPTER 2

	Author	Year	Reference
1			PSAL 2 vi p 438
2	Plint, R.G.	1962	TCWAAS NS LXII p 19
3	Haszeldine, R N and Haszeldine, R. S	2003	Neolithic, natural or new? Critical observations of cup and ring petroglyphs in Langdale, Cumbria. TCWAAS 3rd Series Vol III pp 1-21.
4	Ibid.		
5	Brown,P and Brown, P.M.	1999	Archaeology North 16 Some unrecorded prehistoric rock carving at Copt Howe, Chapel Stile, Great Langdale, Cumbria
6	Beckensall, S	1983	Northumberland's Prehistoric Rock Carvings. Pendulum Publications p 17
7	Beckensall, S	1983	op. cit. p 26

CHAPTER 3

1 Wainwright,A	1958	The Central Fells Loft Crag 5 Westmorland Gazette

CHAPTER 4

1 Claris, P and Quartermaine, J		op. cit. p 32
2 Plint, R G	1962	Stone Axe Factory Sites in the Cumbrian Fells TCWAAS NS LXII p 13
3 Claris, P and Quartermaine, J		op. cit. p 13

CHAPTER 5

1 Claris, P and Quartermaine, J		op. cit. p 12
2 ibid.		p 6

CHAPTER 6

1 Claris, P and Quartermaine, J		op. cit p 12

CHAPTER 7

1 Claris, P and Quartermaine, J		op. cit. p 11
2 Ibid. pp 9, 11		
3 Ibid. p 11		
4 Ibid. p 11		
5 Ibid. p 7		
6 Ibid. pp 8-9		
7 Ibid. p 8		
8 Ibid. passim		

CHAPTER 8

1 Bradley, R and Edmonds, M.		op. cit. p 138
2 Fell, C	1950	The Great Langdale stone-axe factory TCWAAS L p 7

INDEX